REAL-WORLD MATHEMATICS THROUGH SCIENCE

CLASSIFYING FINGERPRINTS

NANCY COOK

Developed by Washington MESA

DALE SEYMOUR PUBLICATIONS®
Parsippany, New Jersey

D1472598

MESA wishes to express its appreciation to the following people for their advice and assistance, without which this module could not have been completed:

Nancy Cook, Ph.D.
Project Director
Washington MESA
University of Washington
Seattle, Washington

Donna West
Seattle Police Department
Seattle, Washington

Keith Berry, Ph.D.
University of Puget Sound
Tacoma, Washington

Washington MESA middle school mathematics and science teachers in Seattle, Spokane, Tacoma, Toppenish, and Yakima, Washington

Project Editor: Katarina Stenstedt
Production/Manufacturing: Leanne Collins
Design Manager: Jeff Kelly
Text Design: Michelle Taverniti
Cover Design: Dennis Teutschel
Cover Photograph: Geoffrey Gove, The Image Bank

The fingerprints in *Classifying Fingerprints* are reprinted from *The Science of Fingerprints,* U.S. Department of Justice, Federal Bureau of Investigation (Washington, DC, 1985).

Dale Seymour Publications
An imprint of Pearson Learning
299 Jefferson Road, P.O. Box 480
Parsippany, New Jersey 07054-0480
www.pearsonlearning.com
1-800-321-3106

This material in part is based on work supported by Grant No. MDR–8751287 from the National Science Foundation; Instructional Materials Development; 1800 G Street NW; Washington, DC 20550. The material was designed and developed by Washington MESA (Mathematics, Engineering, Science Achievement); 353 Loew Hall FH-18; University of Washington; Seattle, WA 98195. Any opinions, findings, conclusions, or recommendations expressed in this publication are those of Washington MESA and do not necessarily reflect the views of the National Science Foundation.

ISBN 0–201–49310–1
9 10 11 12 13 – DR – 05 04 03 02 01

CLASSIFYING FINGERPRINTS

CONTENTS

Introduction   vii
Conceptual Overview   ix
Activity Overview   x
Materials List   xiii
Resources List   xv

Activity 1. Fingerprints   1

History Link: History of Fingerprinting   8
Technology Link: How to Find the Hidden Print   9
Student Sheet 1.1   Taking Fingerprints   10
Student Sheet 1.2   Me and My Fingerprints   11
Student Sheet 1.3   Analyzing Fingerprints   12–13
Student Sheet 1.4   Fingerprint Patterns   14
Student Sheet 1.5   Galton Characteristics   15

Activity 2. Detective Work   17

Career Link: Forensic Scientists   21
History Link: Juan Vucetich   22
Technology Link: Fingerprints on the High-Tech Highway   23
Student Sheet 2.1   Group Analysis   24
Student Sheet 2.2   Forensic Work   25
Student Sheet 2.3   Who's Who   26
Transparency Master 2.4   Group Analysis   27

Activity 3. Primary Evidence   29

History Link: How Fingerprinting Began a Life of Crime   43
Student Sheet 3.1   Filing Fingerprints   44–46
Student Sheet 3.2   The Henry System   47
Student Sheet 3.3   Classified Information   48
Student Sheet 3.4   Finger Math   49

Transparency Master 3.5   Filing Fingerprints   50
Transparency Master 3.6   Primary Classification of Fingerprints   51

Activity 4. What's in a Number   53

Writing Link: Binary World   60
Student Sheet 4.1   Ten to Two   61–62
Student Sheet 4.2   Binary Primary   63
Student Sheet 4.3   Binary Primary Classification   64
Student Sheet 4.4   More Finger Math   65
Student Sheet 4.5   Binary Systems   66
Transparency Master 4.6   Ten to Two   67

Activity 5. Loops, Arches, and Whorls   69

Interest Link: Frequency of Fingerprint Patterns   73
Writing Link: Other Uses for Fingerprinting   74
Student Sheet 5.1   Classy Patterns   75
Student Sheet 5.2   The LAW   76
Student Sheet 5.3   Women and the LAW   77
Student Sheet 5.4   The Finger of the LAW   78
Student Sheet 5.5   LAW Summary   79

Activity 6. The National Crime Information Center   81

Career Link: FBI Agents   87
Technology Link: Fingerprint Locks   88
Interest Link: Other Methods of "Printing"   89
Student Sheet 6.1   Cores, Deltas, and Ridges   90
Student Sheet 6.2   Pattern Differentiation   91–92
Student Sheet 6.3   NCIC FPC   93
Student Sheet 6.4   NCIC FPC and Me   94
Transparency Master 6.5   Fingerprint Pattern Differentiation   95

Family Activity: Are Whorls Inherited?   97

Interest Link: They Won't Go Away!   101
Writing Link: Write a Mystery   102
Career Link: Donna West   103
Family Activity Sheet 1   Family Patterns   104
Family Activity Sheet 2   Fingerprint Classification   105
Family Activity Sheet 3   Family Whorl Count   106

Completed Student Sheets   107–112

INTRODUCTION

Classifying Fingerprints is one of the middle-grades instructional modules created and field-tested by the Washington MESA (Mathematics, Engineering, Science Achievement) project. Washington MESA operates on the premise that effective classroom materials should facilitate connections between classroom and real-world mathematics and science. Staff members and teachers work with scientists, mathematicians, and engineers to outline each module. Pilot modules are tested in middle school classrooms, then revised using feedback from the teachers.

The modules weave important mathematics themes with relevant, exciting science topics. The activities are based on current reform philosophies recommended by the National Council of Teachers of Mathematics' (NCTM's) *Curriculum and Evaluation Standards for School Mathematics* and the American Association for the Advancement of Science's *Project 2061*. Students will

◆ learn by doing. Students take their own fingerprints and analyze them as they investigate the mathematics of forensic science.

◆ employ a variety of reasoning processes by using several mathematics approaches to solve similar problems.

◆ learn to express technical concepts as they write and discuss answers to open-ended questions. The questions are designed to provoke further thought about how science and mathematics connect to the everyday world.

◆ learn the appropriate use of calculators by solving real problems. Students are taught how to conceptualize and set up problems that they can then solve using calculators.

◆ make connections between mathematics and science as well as within mathematics and science. Writing Link, History Link, Interest Link, and Technology Link activities are included to expand the connections to other subject areas.

◆ explore careers by simulating professional roles in the activities. Students also study jobs that use mathematics and science in the Career Link features.

Classifying Fingerprints directs middle school students toward active involvement in learning. Students emulate real-world work environments by collaborating in small groups and striving for group consensus. They work with concrete materials and evaluate open-ended problems—the combination that helps the transition from concrete to abstract thinking crucial to the intellectual development of students at this age. To ascertain that instruction is working, assessment is integrated into *Classifying Fingerprints* activities. Assessment and instruction goals are identical.

Family encouragement can help students to succeed educationally, so a special activity involves students' families in hands-on, collaborative work. Students learn as they show parents and other family members what they have learned.

Each activity begins with an Overview page summarizing what students will be doing and how the teacher needs to prepare. This is followed by background information for the teacher's use and a Presenting the Activity section, which describes the activity in detail and suggests discussion questions and assessment strategies. This is followed by Student Sheets and Transparency Masters in blackline master form (completed Student Sheets are provided on pages 107–112). Career Link, History Link, Writing Link, Technology Link, and Interest Link features are found throughout the book.

CONCEPTUAL OVERVIEW

Classifying Fingerprints addresses the following mathematics topics, science topics, and NCTM standards.

NCTM Curriculum Standards

Problem Solving
  Open-Ended
  Multiple Strategies
Communication
  Verbal and Written
Reasoning
  Logical and Spatial
  Predictions and Evaluations
Mathematical Connections
  Among Topics
  To Real-World Contexts

NCTM Teaching Standards

Worthwhile Tasks
  Real-World Contexts
Teacher's Role
  Listening and Observing
  Orchestrating Discourse
Enhancement Tools
  Calculators
  Concrete Materials
Learning Environment
  Collaborative Work

NCTM Evaluation Standards

Alignment
  Integral to Instruction
Multiple Sources
  Oral and Written
  Individual and Group
Multiple Methods
  Instructional Planning
  Grading
Mathematical Power
  Communicating
  Reasoning
  Integrating
  Generalizing

Mathematics Content

Number Systems
  Decimal System
  Binary System
Computation and Estimation
  Mental Arithmetic
  Calculations
  Calculators
  Estimation
Patterns and Functions
  Pattern Differentiation
  Pattern Identification

Statistics
  Data Collection
  Data Analysis
  Tables
  Graphs
  Inferences
  Hypothesis Testing
  Correlation

Science Topics

Fingerprints
  Pattern Types
  Galton Characteristics
  Focal Points
  Type Lines
  Biological Factors
Scientific Process
  Hypothesizing
  Analyzing
  Concluding
Classification Systems
  Non-Numerical
  Henry System
  FBI Fingerprint Code
Family Patterns
  Inheritance of Patterns

ACTIVITY OVERVIEW

Overview

Middle school students know about the use of fingerprints in criminal investigations. However, they probably do not know much about the different types of fingerprint patterns or the methods for classifying and filing fingerprints. Since the most widely used method of classifying fingerprints is a binary system, *Classifying Fingerprints* provides an opportunity to study a real-world use of a number system other than the decimal system.

Classifying Fingerprints gives students a sampling of activities that forensic scientists do as well as an introduction to the mathematics involved. Students learn how forensic scientists must be top-notch problem solvers who rely on their perceptive and organizational skills, particularly for pattern recognition and differentiation. They also explore the statistical analysis utilized in all phases of forensic work.

Your local police department may be willing to send a detective or a fingerprint expert, both of whom may have degrees in forensic science, to participate in some part of this module so students can pursue their questions and ideas further. A class visit by a forensic scientist could fit anywhere into the module, and it would especially complement Activity 1.

Activity 1: Fingerprints

Students make a full set of fingerprints as well as duplicate copies of their right index fingerprint to be used in Activity 2. Students are introduced to the procedures involved in analyzing fingerprints and then analyze the prints of their right index finger. Students discover the three types of fingerprint patterns—whorls, loops, and arches. They also discover the Galton characteristics, the specific combination of which makes one's fingerprint unique.

Activity 2: Detective Work

Students learn how a fingerprint examiner or a detective analyzes and determines if two fingerprints match. Each student is given a fingerprint of an unknown classmate (one of the two prints of the right index fingers that each student made during Activity 1), and he or she formally analyzes it. Students immediately become aware of the importance of pattern recognition and differentiation skills in forensic science. The teacher displays the remaining prints that have students' names. When the fingerprint analysis is complete, students search for a match among all the named fingerprints.

Activity 3: Primary Evidence

Students learn how fingerprints were filed and located when they first came into use in the last part of the nineteenth century. The system, although it was not numerical, was a binary system based on the presence or absence of a whorl. The Henry System of Fingerprint Classification is a numerical system that makes the process of filing prints more efficient, and it too is a binary system. Students calculate their Henry number and file their prints based on the Henry number. They also learn how to decode Henry numbers to identify the fingers that have whorls.

Activity 4: What's in a Number?

Students review the base 2 number system and translate their Henry number, which uses base 10 numerals, to a base 2 number. They discover that in base 2 they can identify fingers that have whorls by examining the place value position of each 1. They finish the activity by discussing within their groups the similarities and differences between the two systems, and by writing a brief statement explaining why the Henry System is a binary system, regardless of what types of numerals are employed.

Activity 5: Loops, Arches, and Whorls

It was discovered early in the twentieth century, as the use of fingerprints became more accepted, that the three types of patterns—loops, arches, and whorls—did not occur with the same frequency. Loops account for the vast majority of all fingerprint patterns, with whorls being next, and arches occurring infrequently. The distribution of these patterns as a function of various factors, such as gender and ethnic background, has been studied throughout the years, and the data are contradictory. In this activity, students obtain the pattern type for everyone in the class as a function of gender and finger position. They then analyze and graph the data and write a summary statement on their findings.

Activity 6: The National Crime Information Center

The National Crime Information Center (NCIC) is a computerized informational system established to provide information to all federal, state, and local law enforcement agencies. It maintains numerous files, one of which is the Fingerprint Classification (FPC) file. The information is stored on a computer in the headquarters of the Federal Bureau of Investigation in Washington, D.C., and it is transmitted to agencies in the network by computer communication lines. Students study the various factors included in the NCIC FPC and then determine their NCIC FPC codes.

Family Activity: Are Whorls Inherited?

It has been hypothesized that the type of fingerprint pattern tends to be inherited. That is, the frequency of a particular type of pattern appears to be constant within families. The data to date are contradictory; some research supports the hypothesis, and other research contradicts it. Students work with their family groups in investigating this hypothesis. They obtain the pattern type on each finger for every family member, and they analyze it in terms of parent-offspring patterns.

MATERIALS LIST

The following is a consolidated list of materials needed in *Classifying Fingerprints*. A list of materials needed for each activity is included in the Overview for each activity.

Activity	Materials Required
Fingerprints	*For the teacher:* ◆ Transparencies of Student Sheets 1.3–1.5 (optional) ◆ Paper towels *For each student:* ◆ Student Sheets 1.1–1.5 ◆ Scratch paper ◆ Two 3" × 5" cards ◆ Soft lead pencil ◆ Magnifying glass *For each group of students:* ◆ Clear tape
Detective Work	*For the teacher:* ◆ Transparency Master 2.4 ◆ Pins or tape ◆ Coded fingerprint cards from Activity 1 *For each student:* ◆ Student Sheets 2.1–2.3 ◆ Completed Student Sheets 1.4–1.5 ◆ Magnifying glass

Activity	Materials Required
Primary Evidence	*For the teacher:* ◆ 2 copies of Transparency Master 3.5 ◆ Transparency Master 3.6 ◆ 3 clear transparency sheets ◆ 5 pens in different colors *For each student:* ◆ Student Sheets 3.1–3.4 ◆ Completed Student Sheet 1.2 ◆ Magnifying glass
What's in a Number?	*For the teacher:* ◆ Transparency Master 4.6 ◆ A transparency of Student Sheet 4.1 *For each student:* ◆ Student Sheets 4.1–4.5 ◆ Completed Student Sheet 3.2
Loops, Arches, and Whorls	*For the teacher:* ◆ Transparencies of Student Sheets 5.1, 5.3, and 5.4 *For each student:* ◆ Student Sheets 5.1–5.5 ◆ Completed Student Sheet 3.2
The National Crime Information Center	*For the teacher:* ◆ Transparency Master 6.5 ◆ A transparency of Student Sheet 6.1 ◆ A transparency of ridge-count diagram in Background Information (optional) *For each student:* ◆ Student Sheets 6.1–6.4 ◆ Completed Student Sheet 1.2 ◆ Magnifying glass
Family Activity	*For the teacher:* ◆ A transparency of Family Activity Sheet 3 *For each student:* ◆ Presenting the Activity pages ◆ Family Activity Sheets 1–3 ◆ Completed Student Sheets 1.1–1.2 ◆ Magnifying glass

RESOURCES LIST

This list of resources was compiled by teachers, scientists, and professionals who participated in developing *Classifying Fingerprints*. It is intended for teachers who would like to pursue the topic further with their classes, for small groups of students who are particularly interested in the topic, for individual students who desire further investigations, or for the teacher's own professional development.

Cummins and Midlo. *Finger Prints, Palms and Soles.* Philadelphia: The Blakiston Company, 1943.

Frederick Kuhne. *The Finger Print Instructor.* New York: Munn and Company, 1916.

Galton, Francis. *Finger Prints.* 1892. Reprint, New York: Da Capo Press, Inc., 1966.

Henry, Edward R. *Classification and Uses of Fingerprints.* 1916. Reprint, New York: AMS Pr., 1974.

Knill, George. "Fingerprints and Fractions." *The Mathematics Teacher,* November, 1980.

Knill, George. "Mathematics in Forensic Science." *The Mathematics Teacher,* February 1981.

Penrose, L. S. "Dermatoglyphics." *Scientific American,* December 1969.

U.S. Department of Justice, Federal Bureau of Investigation, Superintendent of Documents. *The Science of Fingerprints.* Rev. ed. Washington, D.C.: GPO, 1985.

Young, Sharon L. "Fingerprint Classification." *Arithmetic Teacher,* March 1991.

ACTIVITY

1

FINGERPRINTS

Overview

Students make a full set of fingerprints as well as two additional prints of their right index finger to be used in Activity 2. They then learn how to analyze a fingerprint.

Time. One 40- to 50-minute period.

Purpose. Students discover the main types of fingerprint patterns as well as many of the specific characteristics that make up these patterns.

Materials. *For the teacher:*

◆ Transparencies of Student Sheets 1.3–1.5 (optional)

◆ Paper towels

For each student:

◆ Student Sheets 1.1–1.5

◆ Scratch paper

◆ Two 3" × 5" cards

◆ Soft lead pencil

◆ Magnifying glass

For each group of students:

◆ Clear tape

Getting Ready

1. Duplicate Student Sheets 1.1–1.5.

2. Prepare transparencies of Student Sheets 1.3–1.5 (optional).

3. Prepare secret code system (see Background Information).

4. Locate scratch paper, soft pencils if necessary, tape, 3" × 5" cards, paper towels, and magnifying glasses.

Background Information

In this activity, students learn how to take fingerprints and begin to investigate the techniques and patterns used in fingerprint identification. Using magnifying glasses, students examine their index fingerprints and learn how to differentiate identifying characteristics. Students will be familiar with the idea of fingerprints and their importance in forensics. Some students might have made their fingerprints before, but many will not have.

Fingerprints are formed because the skin on the end of the finger is not smooth. It consists of ridges and valleys. The ridges (the raised parts) leave impressions, and the valleys (the non-raised parts) do not. It is the configuration of these ridges and valleys on your finger that is known as your *fingerprint pattern*.

There are three general categories of fingerprint patterns. Within each pattern, there are numerous variations.

The Three Types of Fingerprint Patterns

Pattern	Examples		
Whorl			
Loop			
Arch			

The three general patterns are whorls, loops, and arches. Whorls are swirly patterns consisting of a series of irregular circles or spirals around a central core. In a whorl, the ridges have no identifiable end. Loops look like opened whorls—parts of concentric circles are somewhat squashed and surround a core. In a loop, the ridges are formed around a core as in a whorl, but they do not close forming spirals. Rather, the ridges enter from one side of the finger, curve around the core, and leave the finger on the same side from which they entered. Arches, on the other hand, do not curve back upon themselves at all. In an arch, the ridges enter from one side of the fingerprint and exit on the other side. The chart above shows some typical whorls, loops, and arches.

In addition, there are five basic characteristics that are present in most fingerprints, and it is the relation among these characteristics, some in multiple counts, that makes a fingerprint unique. The five characteristics are the fork (or bifurcation), the dot, the ending ridge, the enclosure, and the short ridge. These characteristics frequently occur in combinations. All of them, including the compound characteristics, are called *Galton Characteristics*—named after the famous biologist Sir Francis Galton who contributed much of the pioneering work on fingerprints. The five basic Galton characteristics are shown below. Note that the characteristics' names indicate the shape.

Five Galton Characteristics

Galton Characteristic	Example
Fork (Bifurcation)	
Dot	
Ending Ridge	
Enclosure	
Short Ridge	

Fingerprints have two further identifying points, called *focal points*—the delta and the core. The delta consists of a fork and a nearby ridge or dot. It acquired its name from the fact that in most cases the fork in the delta and the nearest ridge to it appear to form a triangle, which is the shape of the Greek letter delta. All whorls have two or more deltas, loops have one, and arches have no delta.

The core of the whorl is unmistakable; it is the center circle, or the core of the spiral. The core of the loop is either the bend of the innermost ridge of the loop, the part of the innermost ridge that curves back in the direction from which it came, or it is the end of the innermost ridge if the ridge stops rather than bends back. Arches have no cores. The diagram below identifies the core and the two deltas in a whorl and the core and the delta in a loop.

The Core and Deltas in Examples of Whorl and Loop Patterns

Pattern	Example
Whorl	Delta — [fingerprint image] — Core, Delta
Loop	Delta — [fingerprint image] — Core

Teachers report that the easiest and most reliable method for producing a high-quality fingerprint consists of these steps:

◆ Use a soft pencil to color a patch on a piece of scratch paper large enough to cover the surface of the finger.

◆ Rub the finger in the graphite on the paper, rocking it from side to side.

◆ Take a short piece of wide, clear tape and wrap it around the part of the finger that is covered with graphite.

◆ Carefully remove the tape from the finger and tape it onto the official record.

The fingerprints made with tape will be a mirror image of prints made using the standard police or FBI method. When the police or FBI take a print, they place the finger on a smooth metal or glass surface that has been coated with a thin film of black ink. They then press the inked finger directly on the fingerprint form. Note that making fingerprints with tape has an extra step—the print is put on the tape, then the tape is put on the form. This results in a print that is a mirror image to one that has been put directly onto the form. Discuss this with the students. Have them do a print of the same finger using each method and compare the two.

Whether or not the prints are mirror images of standard FBI prints does not affect the work done in *Classifying Fingerprints;* however, it should be mentioned for accuracy in relation to the real-world use of fingerprints. You may want to tape the prints on a piece of clear mylar, such as a blank overhead sheet, so they can be viewed from either perspective.

Student Sheet 1.1 gives the procedure for making fingerprints. Students will need time to experiment with the procedure in order to produce high-quality prints. Some students will master the technique quickly, others will take more time.

Student Sheet 1.1 also instructs each student to make two prints of his or her right index finger. Students should do this activity first, because these prints are needed for Activity 2. Everyone should make prints of the right index finger to minimize external clues in the matching of prints. When students complete this activity, they should begin Student Sheet 1.2, which provides space for their full set of fingerprints.

As students complete their sets of index fingerprints, they will bring them to you. One fingerprint card will have the student's name on it, and you are to secretly code the matching card. One way to code the cards is to use the number by each student's name in your grade book, or have a number code ready before class begins. The coding process will go smoothly if you have ready access to a code that includes each student's name and a preassigned number. Do not number them in the order in which they are brought to you.

Student Sheet 1.3 gives an example of a partially-analyzed print and a brief overview of the process. Student Sheet 1.4 gives examples of whorls, loops, and arches; Student Sheet 1.5 gives examples of the five basic characteristics. Students, working in small groups, should ensure that members of their groups understand the process of analyzing prints as they work. This is in preparation for Activity 2, which has students analyze prints to find the match.

The History Link "History of Fingerprints" and the Technology Link "How to Find the Hidden Print" may be used at any time to spark student interest.

Presenting the Activity

Taking Fingerprints. Divide students into small working groups. Four to a group works well for this activity. Ask:

◆ What do you know about fingerprints?

◆ Has anyone in the class ever made their fingerprints?

◆ If anyone has, how did you do it and what were the results?

◆ Has anyone used a different method?

Without telling them any more about fingerprints, explain the task at hand. Each student is to make two prints of his or her right index finger, putting one on each of two cards. When handing out the cards, decide on an orientation that will be used by all to minimize external clues. Either orientation is satisfactory, as long as all students use the same one.

Review the procedure and point out that it is given on the handout. Show students where to wrap the tape so they obtain a full print, not just the print of the tips of their fingers. Tell students to write their names on just one card, and then bring both cards to you to secretly code. Explain that in Activity 2, the cards with names will be displayed around the room, and each student will receive a card with a number. Their tasks will be to determine whose prints they were given.

Explain that when they finish with the index fingerprints, they will begin making a full set of prints. Hand out Student Sheet 1.1, cards, magnifying glasses, and tape. Have scratch paper available and soft pencils to loan to those who do not have ready access to one. Move around the room to make sure everyone is taking good prints—prints that are clear when observed with a magnifying glass. Have paper towels ready for students to clean their fingers during the process and when they are done.

Coding the Cards. Have your code ready! As students bring their pairs of cards to you, check that both prints are clear, that only one has a name on it, and that the name is in clear view. Check the back of the cards to make sure students are not accidentally putting their name there. If they did, have them redo it. Code the cards and separate them into two groups— named cards and coded cards.

As you take students' pairs of cards, give them Student Sheet 1.2. Students should have no difficulty taking a full set of prints, once they have successfully completed taking the prints of their index fingers.

Analyzing Fingerprints. As students are ready, hand out Student Sheets 1.3–1.5. Have students work in groups to help each other learn the process of identifying and labeling the different patterns and characteristics. The most difficult characteristic to identify is the delta, so move from group to group to make sure students are coming to consensus on the deltas. Student Sheet 1.3 allows students to refine their observation skills. If students do not have time to finish this sheet in class, have them finish it for homework. However, make sure they do make another print of their index finger on Student Sheet 1.3 before they go home. Activity 2 begins with a class discussion of what students discovered as they worked through Student Sheet 1.3.

Have students keep Student Sheets 1.4 and 1.5 to use as a reference in Activity 2, or collect these sheets and hand them out when you hand out Student Sheet 2.2. After students have had a chance to analyze the print on Student Sheet 1.3, use a transparency of it to orchestrate a discussion of the process to ensure that all the students understand it.

Discussion Questions

1. What did you notice about your fingerprints? Did any one print look similar to another? Could you clearly tell one from another? Explain.

2. Describe the different patterns you observed. Did they occur with the same frequency or did you see more of one type pattern? Explain. Check to see what other members of your group observed.

3. Has anyone ever seen an official police set of fingerprints in a magazine or newspaper?

4. How do you think the FBI identifies fingerprints?

Assessment Questions

1. Analyze the print of the little finger on your left hand in as much detail as possible. Label each characteristic.

2. List all the different characteristics or patterns that were observed by your group. Did any of the characteristics occur close to each other? Describe any such findings.

3. Propose a procedure to be used in matching fingerprints.

History of Fingerprinting

More than three thousand years ago in Babylonia, a businessman finished recording an important document on soft clay. To protect it against forgery, he pressed his fingers into the clay to leave his prints. Did he know that his print was a unique "signature"? Researchers do not know if fingerprints were really understood in ancient times. But they do know that humans were aware of the amazingly unique patterns of ridges spiraling and curving on their fingers.

For example, at the edge of a lake in Nova Scotia, there is an ancient American Indian rock carving. The picture is an outline of a hand showing the ridge patterns on the hand and fingers—including a whorl pattern on the thumb. And in France, off the coast of Brittany, there is an ancient burial passage covered with designs that look like whorls, loops, and arches from fingerprints.

By the third century B.C., the Chinese were already using single fingerprints as "seals" for important documents. One side of the seal was impressed with the person's name. The other side showed their thumb print. The Japanese used thumb prints to sign documents until 1860. Researchers do not know if these ancient users of fingerprints were using the prints as identification, or if the prints were simply "personal marks" to make the documents seem more binding.

Italian professor Marcello Malpighi was probably the first to notice how the ridges on people's fingertips formed patterns. This was in 1686. No one paid any attention to his findings until 1823 when another professor, John Purkinje, began classifying the ridge patterns into nine varieties.

It wasn't until the turn of the twentieth century that fingerprinting for police identification began in England and Wales. Fingerprints have now become important tools used most often to identify criminals and victims of accidents.

How to Find the Hidden Print

You are a criminalist who has just arrived on the scene of a murder. The police have roped off the area to prevent anyone from destroying evidence. You look around carefully. It appears the murderer did not leave any visible prints. But more likely than not, there are invisible prints—called *latent* fingerprints— because, like all of us, the culprit had a bit of perspiration and oil on each fingertip. Anything he or she touched would bear a hidden fingerprint that can be revealed with the proper equipment.

The most common way to find latent prints is to "dust" for them. From your fingerprint dusting kit, you pull out two jars of powder. You will use the gray powder on dark-colored surfaces and the black powder on light-colored surfaces. You look around the room for any glass, metal, or mirrors the murderer might have touched (the dusting method only works on nonporous materials such as these). With the tip of a camel-hair brush, you gently brush some powder on the window the murderer supposedly entered through. If there is a print there, the powder will stick to the oil in the prints. You would then press a piece of tape against the powder to lift the print. Unfortunately, you find no prints on the window.

Your next approach is to try to chemically develop latent prints from porous articles such as unpainted wood, cloth, and paper. For this you use iodine or silver nitrate. You do find some prints using this method, but they are smudged.

Your last hope for finding a usable fingerprint lies in laser technology. The lasers work by making the waste molecules in perspiration glow, or *fluoresce.*

A week later in the forensic laboratory, using laser equipment, you find several fingerprints on the victim's shirt. You input the fingerprints into a special computer file that zips through millions of fingerprints and compares them to the prints you found. Minutes later, the computer tells you it has found several possible matches, one of which is a 99 percent match. Quickly you pick up the phone to call the investigator in charge of the case—"I think we've found the murderer," you say. . . .

Taking Fingerprints

Procedure for taking a fingerprint:

◆ Using a soft pencil, number 1 or 2, color a patch large enough to cover the surface of your finger on a piece of scratch paper. A patch one inch square will usually do.

◆ Rub your finger in the graphite on the paper. Roll your finger from side to side to get a full print.

◆ Take a short piece of clear tape—about 1-inch long—and wrap it around the part of your finger that is covered with graphite. Carefully remove the tape from your finger and put it on the paper. You should have a clear fingerprint under the tape. Do not remove the tape.

◆ Note: The print taped on the paper is a mirror image of the print as it would appear in the FBI files. If you tape it on plastic, you can turn the plastic over to view it as it would appear on a legal form.

You will need to experiment. The goal is to get a print in which you can see all the ridges (lines) very clearly when viewing the print with a magnifying glass.

1. Practice making a fingerprint of your right index finger on scratch paper.

2. When you think you have the technique mastered, make two fingerprints of your right index finger and tape one on each of two 3" × 5" cards in the correct orientation.

3. Write your name on one and only one of the cards. Give both cards to your teacher at the same time. Your teacher is going to secretly code your prints.

4. When you have both cards made and accepted by your teacher, pick up a copy of Student Sheet 1.2 and begin making a complete set of fingerprints.

Me and My Fingerprints

1. Using the procedure described on Student Sheet 1.1, practice taking your fingerprints on scratch paper.

2. When you have the technique mastered, complete the fingerprint chart below.

	Thumb	Index	Middle	Ring	Little
Right Hand					

	Thumb	Index	Middle	Ring	Little
Left Hand					

When you have a complete set of clear fingerprints, begin work on Student Sheet 1.3.

Analyzing Fingerprints

1. An example of a partially-analyzed fingerprint is given below. Note the method of identifying a characteristic, labeling it in the margins, and drawing a line between the characteristic and the label.

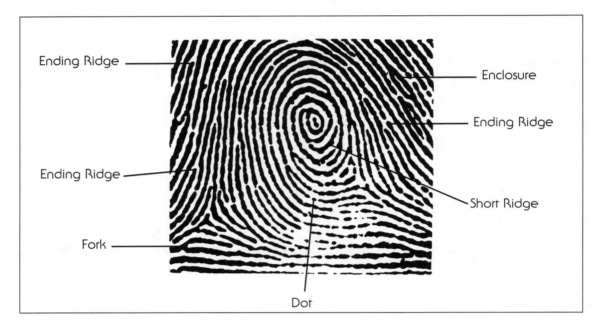

Ending Ridge

Enclosure

Ending Ridge

Ending Ridge

Short Ridge

Fork

Dot

2. Student Sheet 1.4 illustrates the three types of fingerprint patterns. The above fingerprint has what type pattern?

3. Student Sheet 1.5 illustrates the different types of characteristics. Referring to it, continue the analysis of the print above by identifying and labeling at least five other characteristics. (You do not have to use all five *types* of characteristics.)

Analyzing Fingerprints

4. Make a new fingerprint of your right index finger in the middle of the space below. Using a magnifying glass, identify and label its characteristics.

My Right Index Fingerprint

5. What pattern is it?

6. Summarize your findings.

Fingerprint Patterns

Pattern	Examples		
Whorl			
Loop			
Arch			

Galton Characteristics

Characteristic	Example
Fork (Bifurcation)	
Dot	
Ending Ridge	
Enclosure	
Short Ridge	

ACTIVITY 2

DETECTIVE WORK

Overview

Each student is given a classmate's fingerprint card, but the fingerprint owner's identify is unknown. Students analyze their cards and identify whom each card belongs to by matching it to one of the name-identified fingerprints that are displayed around the room.

Time. Two 40- to 50-minute periods.

Purpose. Students gain knowledge of the patterns and characteristics that contribute to the uniqueness of fingerprints. They strengthen their perceptive skills and pattern recognition.

Materials. *For the teacher:*

◆ Transparency Master 2.4

◆ Pins or tape

◆ Coded fingerprint cards from Activity 1

For each student:

◆ Student Sheets 2.1–2.3

◆ Completed Student Sheets 1.4–1.5

◆ Magnifying glass

Getting Ready

1. Duplicate Student Sheet 2.1–2.3.
2. Prepare Transparency Master 2.4.
3. Locate pins or tape, fingerprint cards, and magnifying glasses.
4. Locate Student Sheets 1.4–1.5 (unless students kept them from Activity 1).

Background Information

This activity continues the work begun in Activity 1. Students refine and employ forensic investigative techniques. In Activity 1, students became familiar with fingerprint patterns and characteristics as they analyzed their own fingerprints. In this activity, students formalize the process of fingerprint analysis, and then use the procedure to analyze classmates' fingerprints.

Transparency Master 2.4 gives an enlarged copy of the fingerprint on Student Sheet 2.1. Use the transparency to have the class work through the process of analyzing a fingerprint. You do not need to do a complete analysis; continue until you feel all groups are able to identify the different characteristics. Stress the importance of clearly labeling each characteristic—trying to put the label in such a position so as not to have any lines crossing one another.

On Student Sheet 2.2, students practice using the newly-established procedure for analyzing fingerprints. As students analyze the fingerprints on the cards, display the fingerprints with names around the room. Teachers report it is best to spread the prints out so two or three students can observe a print at the same time. You might facilitate crowd control by grouping the prints by general pattern. For example, you might put all the whorls on one wall, all the loops on another wall, and all the arches on another wall. It is best not to give a student his or her own print. Try to have a system that allows you to avoid this without students knowing. It is best to take time before class to preassign the unknown fingerprints. You will then be able to quickly pass them out.

Student Sheet 2.3 provides space for students to record their matches. After a student makes a match, have him or her exchange prints with a member in the group to check each other's matches. The group is to reach consensus on all identifications, and Student Sheet 2.3 provides space to check the work of all members in the group.

Leave enough time for class discussion. Students will want to share their findings. The Career Link "Forensic Scientists," the History Link "Juan Vucetich," and the Technology Link "Fingerprints on the High-Tech Highway" may be used at any time to stimulate student interest.

Presenting the Activity

Group Analysis. Divide students into small working groups. Four to a group works well for this activity. Hand out Student Sheet 2.1, magnifying glasses, and, if they do not have them already, Student Sheets 1.4–1.5. Using Transparency 2.4, work through the initial steps of identifying and labeling the characteristics in the print. The first piece of information to elicit from the group is the pattern type of the print. Then ask someone to point out a characteristic and label it. This could be done by having individual students come to the overhead projector. Stress the importance of organizing the labeling to minimize any confusion. The labeled characteristics are easier to identify when no lines between them and their labels cross. When you feel that students are ready, have them continue in their groups.

Forensic Work. Hand out a numbered fingerprint card to each student. Explain to the class that they are to analyze the prints they were given and then identify whose they are by matching them to one of the prints with a name that you will display around the room.

Hand out Student Sheet 2.2. Instruct each student to analyze the print of the unknown classmate in enough detail that the student can do their "detective work" quickly and efficiently. Students can either do the analysis of the print right on the card, or note the print's highlights on Student Sheet 2.2. Either method works well. It is more efficient to do the analysis on the card, but students who do not have good small-muscle control could produce an analysis that would make the matching task difficult. Discuss the advantages and disadvantages, and let students do whichever they prefer. They will know which is best based on their work from the day before. While students are doing their analyses, use pins or tape to display around the room the cards with names on them.

Who's Who. As students are ready, examine their analyses, and if they contain sufficient detail, give students Student Sheet 2.3. Explain to students they are to identify the owner of the print they analyzed, and then exchange prints with a group member and identify that print also.

Students will most likely identify the one print given them, but the group might not reach consensus on all four identifications. You might want to display the named cards the following day to allow those who did not finish additional time to work.

Leave time to discuss their observations and findings, or plan for discussion time tomorrow.

Discussion Questions

1. What did you notice about the fingerprint given to you? Describe something it had in common with a fingerprint given to a member of your group. Describe a difference.

2. Describe the different characteristics or patterns your group observed.

3. Which types of prints do you think are the most difficult to identify?

Assessment Questions

1. Analyze a fingerprint with enough detail to carry out an efficient investigation.

2. How much detail do you think is necessary in an analysis to make a sure identification? Explain.

3. Describe a procedure for matching fingerprints.

Forensic Scientists

Forensic scientists, also known as *criminalists,* use science to solve crimes. They use fingerprints, DNA from skin cells, handwriting samples, or other clues to help convict criminals.

Criminalists may specialize in one field of forensic science or they may have expertise in many of the fields. Here are a few of the specialized branches of forensic science:

◆ *Forensic pathologists* usually work for the medical examiner's or coroner's office and often perform autopsies to learn the cause of death. A forensic pathologist may be asked to compare the blood of a suspect to blood from a stain.

◆ A *forensic psychiatrist* deals with the minds of criminals. A forensic psychiatrist may be asked to determine if a suspect is legally sane.

◆ If someone has been poisoned or drugged, a *forensic toxicologist* may try to determine what the substance is and what effects it had.

◆ A *forensic ballistics* expert examines bullets, bullet holes, and guns for clues.

◆ A *forensic anthropologist* can often identify the sex, race, age, blood type, and time of death of a victim who has died by studying his or her bones. Sometimes, a forensic anthropologist can recreate what the face of the person looked like based on the shape of the skull.

Criminalists work in crime laboratories, usually run by the federal, state, or local government. To be a criminalist, you need a college degree in chemistry or criminalistics. Some schools offer graduate programs in forensic science.

Juan Vucetich

Juan Vucetich was a well-respected police official in Argentina. One day in 1880, he read an article written by Dr. Henry Faulds that told how no two people have the same fingerprints. Dr. Faulds thought fingerprints would be a excellent way to identify criminals who leave prints at the scene of a crime. Most police agencies in the world did not pay much attention to the article, but it fascinated Vucetich. He began investigating the idea. He even went to the local museum and discovered that the mummies still had tiny lines on their fingers!

In 1892, one of Vucetich's detectives was examining the scene of a murder and noticed that the murderer had left a bloody palm print on the door frame of the house. By comparing the palm print to those of the two suspects in the crime, the detectives were able to identify the murderer and solve a crime using prints for the first time in history.

After much research, Vucetich developed a way to classify fingerprints so his police could use them. Juan Vucetich's classification system is still used in most Spanish-speaking countries.

Fingerprints on the High-Tech Highway

In San Francisco in 1978, a woman was shot and killed by a burglar. The police found three fingerprints. It was the job of the investigator at the scene of the crime to check the prints against those on file. The problem: there were 400,000 files in the San Francisco Police Department. Six years later the investigator was still searching for the killer, and there were still 100,000 prints to look at.

Then in 1984, the San Francisco Police Department installed one of the first Automated Fingerprint Identification Systems (AFISs). The inspector fed a tracing of the fingerprints into this computer and found an extremely close match. Two days later the alleged killer was arrested, and soon after, he confessed. In the next few years the San Francisco police solved over 2,000 cases that had been unsolved because print matches had not yet been found.

More than half the 50 states now have AFIS technology. Devices are now able to scan the prints from file cards or the crime scene. The scans are fed into a computer, which makes a detailed "map" of the print, codes it, and puts it in memory. When a detective asks the computer to compare a scan to files on memory, the computer looks for and lists all possible matches. Each name on the list has a score based on how closely the match fits.

Group Analysis

1. As a group, analyze this print. Discuss any discrepancies and work toward consensus.

2. When all groups are ready, the class will discuss the process of analyzing a fingerprint to verify all are using the same procedure. Be prepared to share your findings, particularly your methods to solve discrepancies.

Forensic Work

1. Your teacher will give you a card with a fingerprint of the right index finger of one of your classmates. The card has a number on it. The matching fingerprint is on a card with the person's name on it. You are to analyze the fingerprint and then determine whose it is.

2. Using a magnifying glass, examine the index fingerprint. What pattern does it have?

3. Using a magnifying glass, analyze the print, noting and labeling as many identifying characteristics as you think necessary. If there is not enough space on the card, use the space below to sketch the identifying characteristics.

Someone's Right Index Fingerprint

4. When you have completed the analysis, begin work on Student Sheet 2.3.

Who's Who

1. You have a card with a fingerprint of one of your classmates. The card has a number on it. The matching fingerprint is on a card with the person's name on it. You are to determine whose fingerprint is on the card.

2. Using a magnifying glass and referring to the analysis you have done, search for the matching fingerprint. When you think you have identified the person, exchange cards and Student Sheets 2.2 (if necessary) with someone in your group, and identify the owner of the fingerprint on the new card.

3. Your group is to reach consensus on the identity of the fingerprint on each card your group has. If there is a conflict, decide how to determine whose fingerprint it is.

4. When your group reaches consensus, give the matching number/name pairs to your teacher.

5. Keep a record of the identifications for later discussion by filling out the table below. Record and describe anything that helped you in making the identification.

Number	Name	Description and Comments

Group Analysis

ACTIVITY
3

PRIMARY EVIDENCE

Overview

Students file their fingerprints according to the original system developed in the late nineteenth century. They then learn the Henry System, which was developed to make the filing process more efficient. They determine their primary classification and file their prints based on their classification index.

Time. Two 40- to 50-minute periods.

Purpose. The primary fingerprint classification system is a binary system based on the presence or absence of whorls. Students discover how it greatly simplifies filing and locating sets of fingerprints.

Materials. *For the teacher:*

◆ 2 copies of Transparency Master 3.5

◆ Transparency Master 3.6

◆ 3 clear transparency sheets

◆ 5 pens in different colors

For each student:

◆ Student Sheets 3.1–3.4

◆ Completed Student Sheet 1.2

◆ Magnifying glass

Getting Ready

1. Duplicate Student Sheets 3.1–3.4.

2. Prepare Transparency Masters 3.5–3.6 (make two of 3.5).

3. Locate clear transparency sheets, pens, and magnifying glasses.

4. Locate each student's completed Student Sheet 1.2 (unless students kept them from Activity 1).

Background Information

In this activity, students investigate a real-world use of a binary system. The primary classification system of fingerprints was developed in the last decade of the nineteenth century, in part to provide an efficient method to store and locate fingerprint files.

When fingerprints were first adopted for use in England, they were filed in a large 32 × 32 cubicle cabinet, a cabinet that had 32 × 32 = 1,024 storage slots. An elaborate key was developed to determine the placement of sets of fingerprints within this cabinet. The system was based on the number and location of whorls contained within the fingerprint set.

In this system, the ten fingers are numbered 1 to 10. The thumb on the right hand is called finger 1, the right index finger is called finger 2, and so on. The assigned numbers appear in the upper left corner of a fingerprint form, an example of which is given below.

Sample Fingerprint Form

	1 Thumb	2 Index	3 Middle	4 Ring	5 Little
Right Hand	A	W	L	L	L

	6 Thumb	7 Index	8 Middle	9 Ring	10 Little
Left Hand	W	W	L	L	L

The fingers are further grouped into pairs. The right thumb and index finger make up pair one, and the right middle and ring fingers make up pair two. Pair three consists of the right little finger and left thumb, pair four is made up of the left index and middle fingers, and the left ring and little fingers make pair five. Note each pair consists of one odd finger and one even finger.

The fingerprint pattern type is recorded on the form, *W* for whorl, *L* for loop, and *A* for arch. However, for the filing system, only whorls were considered. The filing system was reduced to W for "whorl" and L for "not whorl," that is, for both loops and arches!

The initial filing system consisted of dividing the filing cabinet into four squares, and then dividing each of those squares into four smaller squares, and so on until you could no longer subdivide the square. Student Sheet 3.1 shows what the cabinet looked like. The 32 slot by 32 slot cabinet was divided into four 16 slot × 16 slot squares. Each of these 16 slot × 16 slot squares was subdivided into four 8 slot × 8 slot squares, and each of these squares was further subdivided into four 4 slot × 4 slot squares. The 4 slot × 4 slot squares were then subdivided into four 2 slot × 2 slot squares, and these were further subdivided into four 1 slot × 1 slot squares, or four boxes. There were five subdivisions in all.

At each subdivision, the patterns on a pair of fingers determined in which part of the cabinet the prints would be filed. The patterns of pair one determined which of the four 16 × 16 squares would be used, and the patterns of pair two determined which 8 × 8 within the appropriate 16 × 16 square would be used. The patterns of pair three determined which 4 × 4 square within the appropriate 8 × 8 square would be used, and so on.

At each division, the set of four squares was keyed as follows: the upper left square contained prints with no whorls (*LL*); the upper right square contained prints with no whorls on the odd finger, but with a whorl on the even finger (*LW*); the lower left square contained the prints with a whorl on the odd finger, but no whorls on the even finger (*WL*); and the lower right square was for prints that had whorls on both even and odd fingers (*WW*) (see chart below).

Key for the Binary System Subdivisions

LL	*LW*
WL	*WW*

The filing of the set of prints given in the sample fingerprint form above would be as follows:

1. For pair one (right thumb and index finger), the key = *LW*, and it would be filed somewhere in the upper right 16 × 16 box square.

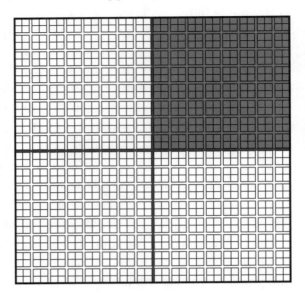

2. For pair two, the key would be *LL*, and the set would be filed somewhere in the upper left 8 × 8 box square within the upper right 16 × 16 box square.

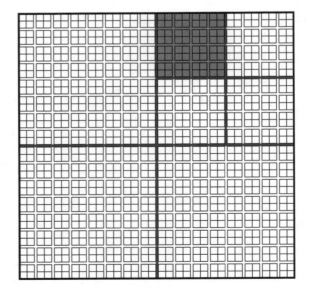

3. The key for pair three would be *LW*, and the set would be filed in the upper right 4 × 4 box square within the assigned 8 × 8 box square.

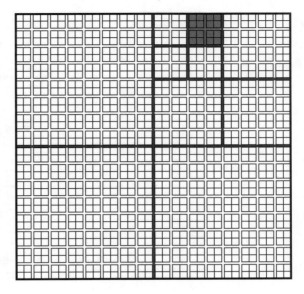

4. The key for pair four would be *WL*, and the set would be filed within the lower left 2 × 2 box square within the assigned 4 × 4 box square.

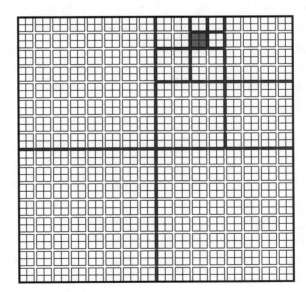

5. The key for pair five would be LL, and the set would be filed in the upper left box within the 2 x 2 box square.

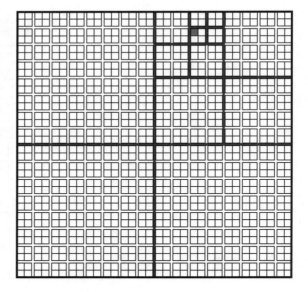

It was a very clever system, and it was a binary system. At each division, the box was determined by the presence or absence of a whorl. The presence or absence of a whorl on the odd finger of a pair determined the vertical position, and the presence or absence of a whorl on the even finger of the pair determined the horizontal position. Finally the idea occurred to Sir Edward Richard Henry to number the boxes and devise a numerical system to identify each box. This became the Henry Primary Classification System.

In this classification system, each finger can have one of two values, a whorl (*W*) or not a whorl (*L*). Each pair of fingers consists of an odd finger and an even finger. Each set of five fingers—odd or even—can have $2^5 = 32$ variations. The following chart lists the 32 variations for odd-numbered fingers.

There are 32 variations for the five odd fingers and 32 variations for the five even fingers. Therefore, the pairs of fingers can be thought of as having $32 \times 32 = 1,024$ variations, which is the exact configuration of the filing cabinet.

Finger					W value	Finger					W value
1	3	5	7	9		1	3	5	7	9	
W	W	W	W	W	31	L	W	W	W	W	15
W	W	W	W	L	30	L	W	W	W	L	14
W	W	W	L	W	29	L	W	W	L	W	13
W	W	W	L	L	28	L	W	W	L	L	12
W	W	L	W	W	27	L	W	L	W	W	11
W	W	L	W	L	26	L	W	L	W	L	10
W	W	L	L	W	25	L	W	L	L	W	9
W	W	L	L	L	24	L	W	L	L	L	8
W	L	W	W	W	23	L	L	W	W	W	7
W	L	W	W	L	22	L	L	W	W	L	6
W	L	W	L	W	21	L	L	W	L	W	5
W	L	W	L	L	20	L	L	W	L	L	4
W	L	L	W	W	19	L	L	L	W	W	3
W	L	L	W	L	18	L	L	L	W	L	2
W	L	L	L	W	17	L	L	L	L	W	1
W	L	L	L	L	16	L	L	L	L	L	0

Knowing that 1 + 2 + 4 + 8 + 16 = 31, which is less than 32 (the number of boxes across or down the filing cabinet), Sir Henry assigned the values to the whorls as follows: a *W* on pair one has a value of 16, a *W* on pair two has a value of 8, a *W* on pair three has a value of 4, a *W* on pair four has a value of 2, and a *W* on pair five has a value of 1. Note the sum of the values assigned even or odd fingers ranges from 0 (no whorls) to 31 (all whorls).

As you can see, each value assigned a whorl is a power of two, thus the Henry System is clearly a binary system. It could be represented by two symbols, for example, 1 and 0, using positional notation, that is, the binary number system.

On a standard fingerprint form, the finger numbers are given in the upper left corner of each box, and the values assigned to whorls appear in the lower right corner of the box, as shown below.

Sample Fingerprint Form with Values Assigned to Whorls

	1 Thumb	2 Index	3 Middle	4 Ring	5 Little
Right Hand	16	16	8	8	4

	6 Thumb	7 Index	8 Middle	9 Ring	10 Little
Left Hand	4	2	2	1	1

The Henry Primary Classification is given as a fraction, and it is calculated by the following formula:

$$\frac{\text{sum of values for whorls of even-numbered fingers} + 1}{\text{sum of values for whorls of odd-numbered fingers} + 1}$$

The cubicles in the filing cases are numbered 1 to 32 in both the horizontal and vertical directions: for the horizontal, the values increase from left to right; for the vertical, the values increase from top to bottom. The value of the even fingers is used to determine the horizontal position, and the value of the odd fingers is used to determine the vertical position.

Note that 1 is added to the numerator and denominator. This is done to enable the numbering of the boxes from 1 to 32 rather than 0 to 31. For example, if there were no whorls on any even-numbered fingers, the sum of the values would be 0, and the numerator would be 1. If a set of prints consisted of all arches and loops, it would have a value of $\frac{1}{1}$ and be filed in box (1,1), the most upper left box in the cabinet, which would agree with the original filing procedure. If a set of prints consisted of all whorls, it would have a value of $\frac{32}{32}$ and be filed in box (32,32), the lowest, furthest right box in the cabinet, also in agreement with the original filing system.

Sample Fingerprints with Values and Patterns Assigned

	1 Thumb	2 Index	3 Middle	4 Ring	5 Little
Right Hand	A 16	W 16	L 8	L 8	L 4

	6 Thumb	7 Index	8 Middle	9 Ring	10 Little
Left Hand	W 4	W 2	L 2	L 1	L 1

In the set of fingerprints given earlier and above, *W* stands for whorl, *A* for arch, and *L* for loop. The primary classification for this set of prints is

$$\frac{16+0+4+0+0+1}{0+0+0+2+0+1} = \frac{21}{3}.$$

There is only one way the values of whorls on even or odd fingers (plus the added 1) could sum to 21, and only one way they could sum to 3. Therefore, there is only one combination of whorls that will yield a primary classification of $\frac{21}{3}$. Once you know the classification value, you know exactly how many whorls there are and exactly where they are. To determine the location of whorls, one works backwards: 21 = 20 + 1; 20 = 16 + 4; therefore, there is a whorl on an even finger that has a whorl value of 16 (finger 2) and a whorl on an even finger that has a whorl value of 4 (finger 6).

The primary classification value is called a fraction, but it is not. It is never reduced; equivalent forms are not applicable. If one were to reduce $\frac{21}{3}$ to $\frac{7}{1}$ the location of whorls could not be uniquely determined, and it might not be filed in the correct box!

Students might not be aware that fingerprints were not immediately accepted as valid identification tools. Before the uniqueness of fingerprints was discovered, there were two primary modes of identification: various body measurements and handwriting. There were problems with both methods. Body measurements can change, particularly with age, and handwriting is also variable, although there are schools of thought today that still consider handwriting a valuable identification technique. More information on the history of fingerprinting is included in the History Link "How Fingerprinting Began a Life of Crime" and Activity 1's History Link "History of Fingerprints."

Student Sheet 3.1 has students file their sets of fingerprints employing the original filing procedure. This may prove difficult for some. You should be prepared to do two or three examples as a class before students attempt it on their own. Student Sheet 3.2 provides space to calculate and record their Henry Primary Classification index. They then file their fingerprints using this numerical index, which is very easy. This facilitates their understanding of the need for efficient numerical systems. Student Sheet 3.3 provides further experience with the Henry System as students determine the Primary Classification index for each member in their group.

Student Sheet 3.4 helps students fully understand that the primary classification index, sometimes called the *Henry Number,* allows one to determine exactly how many whorls there are as well as their locations. The members of one group record their primary classification indexes, and then exchange papers with another group. Students decode the primary index to determine the number and location of whorls for each member of the group.

Presenting the Activity

Filing Fingerprints. Ask students how they think fingerprints were originally stored. Remind them, if necessary, that fingerprints came into use for identification purposes late in the nineteenth century. Elicit from students what type of technology was available at that time. Discuss the use of the 32 × 32 box filing cabinet. Elicit from the class possible procedures to file sets of fingerprints in this 32 × 32 box filing cabinet. As the suggestions arise, share that part of the system with them. For instance, if someone suggests to number the boxes, point out that the initial system did not use numbers. That came later.

Using Transparency Master 3.5, describe the procedure.

1. Point out that each finger is given a number 1 to 10. Go over the number assigned to each finger in the example shown.

2. Explain that the fingers are paired and describe the pairings.

3. Emphasize that the filing is based on the presence or absence of a whorl on each finger. Acknowledge that loops and arches are both treated the same.

4. Illustrate that each pair of fingers is assigned a filing key based on the presence or absence of whorls on each of the two fingers in the pair. Determine the key for each pair in the example.

5. Explain that the filing cabinet consists of 32 rows with 32 slots in each row. It was a 32 slot by 32 slot cabinet.

6. Discuss the general subdivision process of the 32 slot by 32 slot box filing cabinet as detailed in the Background Information. It facilitates understanding if you display each subdivision with a different color of pen. You will need five colors. It also helps to lay a clear transparency on top of the transparency so you do not have to erase between examples. It helps to have a few clear transparencies available if you do not have a roll on your overhead projector. Do not spend too much time on the process in general, even if some students seem confused. The method will become clear as you work through some examples.

7. Work through the example given in the Background Information, or demonstrate using your own fingerprints. The procedure might be initially confusing, but with a few examples, it will become clear. Work through one or two more examples.

Divide students into groups of four. Hand out Student Sheet 3.1 and magnifying glasses. Students will also need Student Sheet 1.2, which has their full sets of prints on it. Have students work in small groups on a common example to ensure everyone in the group understands the process. The directions are given on Student Sheet 3.1, and students can refer to them when necessary. Students then file their own sets of prints. For further experience, have them file each other's sets.

The Henry System. Have the class comment on the filing system. They will most likely report it is confusing, it is easy to make errors, and there is no easy way to check if an error is made. Share with the class that the people who used this system felt the same way, and eventually a numerical system was developed to make the filing of prints less cumbersome and more efficient. The Henry Primary Classification System, named after its developer, Sir Richard Henry, is a numerical method for filing sets of fingerprints resulting in the same filing locations within the 32 × 32 box as the original, non-numerical method.

Using Transparency Master 3.6, discuss the Henry Primary Classification System of Fingerprints with the class.

1. Point out that the system is still based on the presence or absence of a whorl on any finger, and the fingers are still numbered 1 to 10.

2. However, the fingers are no longer paired, and the key is now a numerical key. Describe the values of whorls assigned to each finger, and point out where they are given on the standard fingerprint form.

3. Discuss the calculation of the Henry Number. Point out that the sum of the values of the whorls on the even fingers + 1 make up the numerator, and the sum of the values of the whorls on the odd fingers + 1 make up the denominator.

4. Using the fingerprint set example from Transparency Master 3.5, record the pattern symbols on the form and work through the calculation of the Henry Number.

5. Using a clean copy of Transparency Master 3.5, label across the top of the grid "Even Fingers" and down the left side "Odd Fingers." Then number the cabinet boxes 1 to 32 from left to right, and 1 to 32 from top to bottom. Help the class determine where the set should be filed based on its primary classification index or Henry number.

6. Do not compare the results of both procedures unless it comes up in the discussion. Students are asked to do this on Student Sheet 3.1.

Students might be interested in reading more about Sir Henry at this time. This History Link "How Fingerprinting Began a Life of Crime" may be used now or at any time during this activity.

Hand out Student Sheet 3.2 and have students work in their groups to calculate their primary classification index. Student Sheet 3.2 directs students to label the cabinet given on Student Sheet 3.1. They then file their sets, and if done correctly, discover that both methods yield the same results.

The numerator gives the value for the even fingers and therefore, the horizontal location in the cabinet. The denominator gives the value for the odd fingers and therefore, the vertical location in the cabinet. Recall in the original, non-numerical filing system, the filing at each subdivision was based on a two-symbol key that consisted of the pattern on an odd finger and the pattern on an even finger.

Have students in their groups analyze the two filing systems and discuss why they give the same result. Have one or two groups share their analyses. Students, who are now aware of how tedious and difficult it was to sort or find fingerprints with these manual filing systems, should compare them with the computerized systems of today.

Primary Classified Information. Hand out Student Sheet 3.3. It allows for more practice in computing the primary classification index. Once students record the fingerprint patterns, they can do the calculations for homework.

Finger Math. Students might not fully comprehend that the primary classification index gives the exact location of each and every whorl in any set of fingerprints. Student Sheet 3.4 gives them the opportunity to discover this fact. Students decode primary classification indexes from members of another group to determine the number and precise location of any whorls in the set. Students should be able to develop a method for doing this. A difficulty might arise if they neglect to subtract the 1 from both the numerator and denominator. As you move about the room checking their progress, be prepared to guide them in this direction.

Discussion Questions

1. Why do you think we have fingerprints? Why do we have ridges and valleys? What other types of prints do we have? Toe prints? Do other animals have "prints"?

2. As a group, list as many uses of fingerprints as you can. Be prepared to share your list with the class.

3. When fingerprints were first being used for identification purposes, there were many people who argued they would never replace handwriting as a major tool of identification. Why do you think so many people held this position?

4. Discuss which you think is a more reliable tool today, fingerprints or handwriting. List the reasons used to support your decision.

Assessment Questions

1. Explain why the Henry Primary Classification System results in filing a set of prints in the same box as the original, non-numerical system.

2. Discuss with your group whether the original, non-numerical procedure for filing sets of fingerprints is binary. Be prepared to defend your decision.

3. Discuss with your group why the primary classification system is called a binary system. Explain in writing, using sufficient examples to convince a parent.

4. Modify the primary classification system to make it even better.

How Fingerprinting Began a Life of Crime

Before the late 1800s, police had no way of keeping track of repeat criminals. They simply jotted down general descriptions (hair color, scars, and so on). Then a police clerk named Alphonse Bertillon came up with idea of using measurements to identify criminals. His system worked in most cases, but soon police realized measurements could be unreliable. A slightly inaccurate measurement of someone's ear could make an innocent man appear to be a repeat criminal.

At about this time, Sir William James Herschel in India, Dr. Henry Faulds in Japan, and several others around the world began wondering whether fingerprints could be used to identify criminals. Soon after, Sir Edward Richard Henry created a simple classification system to use in his police department in Bengal. By 1901, fingerprints entered the world of crime fighting in England and Wales. A year later, the United States began using Henry's classification system to identify criminals.

Soon cities began exchanging print records so officers could try to find matches to prints found at crime scenes. In 1924, Congress established the Identification Division of the Federal Bureau of Criminal Identification. The FBI files contained copies of all the fingerprint files in the United States. In 1932, an international fingerprint exchange began.

As you can imagine, the number of fingerprints on file grew and grew. Fingerprinting quickly became the most popular way to identify people (especially criminals). By 1939, the FBI had 10 million fingerprint cards. By 1982, the number had grown to 176 million.

Filing Fingerprints

	1 Thumb	2 Index	3 Middle	4 Ring	5 Little
Right Hand					

	6 Thumb	7 Index	8 Middle	9 Ring	10 Little
Left Hand					

1. The number in the upper left corner of each box is the finger number. For instance, the thumb on the right hand is called finger number 1.

2. Look at your fingerprints on Student Sheet 2.1. Using W for whorl, L for loop, and A for arch, record your fingerprint patterns in the above chart.

3. When fingerprints were first used, they were filed and stored in a 32 × 32 box cabinet based on the following system:

   a. The 32 × 32 box filing cabinet was divided into four 16 × 16 box squares. Then each of these four squares were subdivided into four 8 × 8 box squares. Then each of these were subdivided into four 4 × 4 box squares. Then each of these were subdivided into four 2 × 2 box squares. And the final subdivision (the fifth) resulted with four 1 × 1 box squares (four boxes). On page 46 is a diagram of the cabinet.

   b. The filing "key" at any step is to go to the appropriate square based on the following:

LL	LW
WL	WW

   LL = neither finger has a whorl.
   LW = the odd finger does not have a whorl, but the even finger does.
   WL = the odd finger has a whorl, but the even finger does not.
   WW = both fingers have whorls.

Filing Fingerprints

c. Determine the key for the first pair of your fingers—1 and 2—the right thumb and index finger. The set of prints will be filed in the appropriate square within this cabinet. For instance, if the odd finger (the thumb) has a whorl, but the even finger does not, the prints will be filed within the lower left part of the cabinet.

d. Determine the key for the next pair of fingers—3 and 4—the right middle and ring fingers. Go to the appropriate square within the subdivision.

e. Determine the key for the next pair of fingers—5 and 6—the right little finger and the left thumb. Go to the appropriate square.

f. Determine the key for the next pair of fingers—7 and 8—the left index and middle fingers, and go to the appropriate square.

g. Determine the key for the last pair of fingers—9 and 10—the left ring and little fingers, and file the prints in the appropriate box.

Filing Fingerprints

4. Record the key for each pair of fingers. Determine and label in which box your fingerprints would be filed.

Finger Pair	1 and 2	3 and 4	5 and 6	7 and 8	9 and 10
Key					

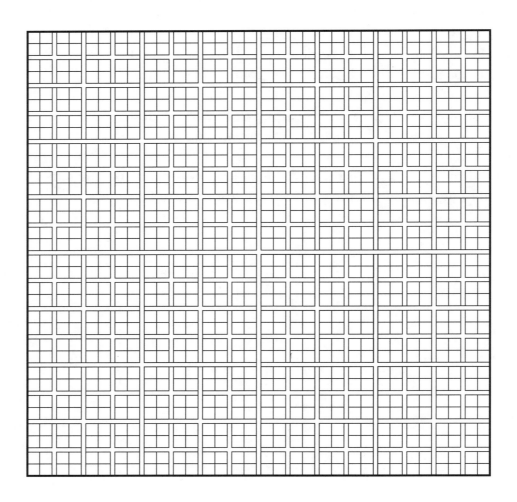

5. Exchange filing charts with a member of your group and check each other's work.

The Henry System

	1 Thumb	2 Index	3 Middle	4 Ring	5 Little
Right Hand	16	16	8	8	4

	6 Thumb	7 Index	8 Middle	9 Ring	10 Little
Left Hand	4	2	2	1	1

1. The number in the upper left corner of each box is the finger number.

2. The number in the lower right corner is the classification value for a whorl.

3. The primary classification of fingerprints is based on the number and location of whorls. No value is given to arches or loops.

4. Primary classification is given as a fraction, and it is calculated by the following formula:

$$\frac{\text{sum of values for whorls of even-numbered fingers} + 1}{\text{sum of values for whorls of odd-numbered fingers} + 1}$$

5. Write the symbol for the pattern observed on each of your fingers in the appropriate box above.

$$W = \text{Whorl} \qquad A = \text{Arch} \qquad L = \text{Loop}$$

6. Calculate your primary classification and record it below.

7. Find the "filing cabinet" on Student Sheet 3.1. Label "Even Fingers" across the top, and number the boxes 1–32 from left to right. Label "Odd Fingers" down the left side, and number the boxes 1–32 from the top to the bottom.

8. File your set of prints using the Henry Primary Classification number. In which box did it go? Where did it go when you used the old, non-numerical system? Explain.

Classified Information

Record the fingerprint patterns for every other member in your group and calculate their primary classifications.

1. Name of group member _____

	1 Thumb	2 Index	3 Middle	4 Ring	5 Little
Right Hand	16	16	8	8	4

	6 Thumb	7 Index	8 Middle	9 Ring	10 Little
Left Hand	4	2	2	1	1

Primary Classification _____

2. Name of group member _____

	1 Thumb	2 Index	3 Middle	4 Ring	5 Little
Right Hand	16	16	8	8	4

	6 Thumb	7 Index	8 Middle	9 Ring	10 Little
Left Hand	4	2	2	1	1

Primary Classification _____

3. Name of group member _____

	1 Thumb	2 Index	3 Middle	4 Ring	5 Little
Right Hand	16	16	8	8	4

	6 Thumb	7 Index	8 Middle	9 Ring	10 Little
Left Hand	4	2	2	1	1

Primary Classification _____

Finger Math

	1 Thumb	2 Index	3 Middle	4 Ring	5 Little
Right Hand	16	16	8	8	4

	6 Thumb	7 Index	8 Middle	9 Ring	10 Little
Left Hand	4	2	2	1	1

1. In the table below, fill in the name and primary classification for each member in your group. Do not fill in the whorl location data.

2. Exchange papers with another group.

3. As a group, determine the whorl locations for each primary classification listed below. Recall that the primary classification is based on the presence or absence of a whorl on each finger. As a group, decide how to work backwards from the primary classification to locate the whorls.

4. When both your group and the group with which you exchanged papers have finished, again exchange papers and check each other's work.

5. As a group, be prepared to explain your decoding system and why it works.

My Group

Name	Primary Classification	Whorl Locations

Filing Fingerprints

	1 Thumb	2 Index	3 Middle	4 Ring	5 Little
Right Hand					

	6 Thumb	7 Index	8 Middle	9 Ring	10 Little
Left Hand					

Finger Pair	1 and 2	3 and 4	5 and 6	7 and 8	9 and 10
Key					

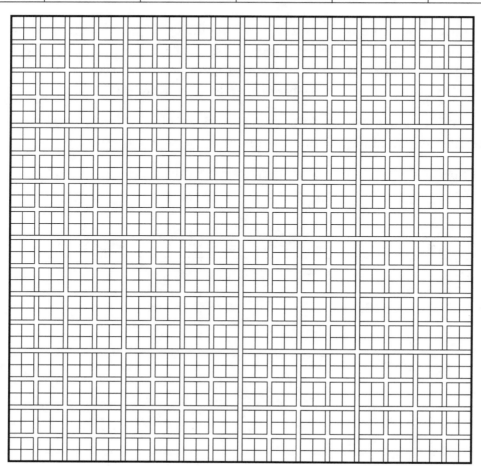

Primary Classification of Fingerprints

	1 Thumb	2 Index	3 Middle	4 Ring	5 Little
Right Hand	16	16	8	8	4

	6 Thumb	7 Index	8 Middle	9 Ring	10 Little
Left Hand	4	2	2	1	1

Primary Classification is given as a fraction.

$$\frac{\text{sum of values for whorls of even-numbered fingers} + 1}{\text{sum of values for whorls of odd-numbered fingers} + 1}$$

ACTIVITY
4

WHAT'S IN
A NUMBER

Overview

The primary fingerprint classification system, although it uses decimal system numerals, is really a binary system based on the presence or absence of a whorl on any finger. The values assigned to whorls are powers of two. Students investigate the binary number system, translate the whorl values to base two, and calculate their Henry Primary Classification in binary.

Time. Two 40- to 50-minute periods.

Purpose. Students review the binary number system in a real-world application by exploring the binary nature of the primary classification system of fingerprints. Such a review will facilitate students' understanding the structure of the decimal system.

Materials. *For the teacher:*

◆ Transparency Master 4.6

◆ A transparency of Student Sheet 4.1

For each student:

◆ Student Sheets 4.1–4.5

◆ Completed Student Sheet 3.2

Getting Ready

1. Duplicate Student Sheets 4.1–4.5.
2. Prepare Transparency Master 4.6.
3. Prepare a transparency of Student Sheet 4.1.
4. Locate each student's completed Student Sheet 3.2 (unless they have them from Activity 3).

Background Information

Middle school students are usually proficient with the decimal system. They are able to carry out the standard operations, and they are able to use the system in problem solving. However, some students might not fully understand the nature of the system itself. For example, they might not comprehend the role of place value. This is not uncommon. One of the best techniques to facilitate further understanding of the decimal system is to study a different but similar system. This activity provides such an opportunity. Students explore a binary number system as they examine the Henry Primary Classification System of fingerprints.

On Student Sheet 4.1, students review the binary number system and translate the first 32 decimal numbers to base 2 numbers. They most likely have done an exercise of this nature before. However, the definition that $2^0 = 1$ might present difficulties for some. The following table gives a pattern that facilitates understanding this definition.

Translation of Sample Decimal Numbers to Base 2 Numbers

Standard Form	Differential in Standard Form	Exponential Form	Differential in Exponent
64		2^6	
32	$\div 2$	2^5	-1
16	$\div 2$	2^4	-1
8	$\div 2$	2^3	-1
4	$\div 2$	2^2	-1
2	$\div 2$	2^1	-1
1	$\div 2$	2^0	-1

In preparation for translating the Henry System to base 2, students review the operation of addition in base 2. All the problems on Student Sheet 4.1 involve the decimal values of whorls—32, 16, 8, 4, 2, and 1—all of which are powers of two. Students will discover that the addition of these selected numbers, the powers of two, are easier in base 2 than in base 10. There is no "carrying"—a feature many students prefer! For example:

Decimal   **Binary**

$16 + 8 = 24$ $10000_2 + 1000_2 = 11000_2$

A profitable discussion may arise when comparing the addition of powers of two in base 2 to the addition of powers of ten in base 10.

Student Sheet 4.2 has students translate the whorl values to base 2. They then use this information to calculate their *binary* primary classification index. In the example below, the binary primary classification index is calculated for the sample set of fingerprints given in Activity 3.

Sample Set of Fingerprints—Decimal Numerals

	1 Thumb	2 Index	3 Middle	4 Ring	5 Little
Right Hand	A 16	W 16	L 8	L 8	L 4

	6 Thumb	7 Index	8 Middle	9 Ring	10 Little
Left Hand	W 4	W 2	L 2	L 1	L 1

The Henry Primary Classification for this set of prints

$$= \frac{16+4+1}{2+1} = \frac{21}{3}$$

Sample Set of Fingerprints Translated to Binary Numerals

	1 Thumb	2 Index	3 Middle	4 Ring	5 Little
Right Hand	A 10000_2	W 10000_2	L 1000_2	L 1000_2	L 100_2

	6 Thumb	7 Index	8 Middle	9 Ring	10 Little
Left Hand	W 100_2	W 10_2	L 10_2	L 1_2	L 1_2

The binary primary classification for this set of prints

$$= \frac{10000_2 + 100_2 + 1_2}{10_2 + 1_2} = \frac{10101_2}{11_2}$$

With practice, students will realize that the positions of 1s in the binary classification system directly identify the locations of whorls. After the "added-on 1" has been subtracted, the 1s in the numerator identify the location of whorls on the even fingers—2, 4, 6, 8, 10—in that order left to right. Recall that the only even finger that can have a value 10000_2 is finger 2. So a 1 in the fifth position to the left identifies a whorl on finger 2. There is no other way to have a 1 in that position on the numerator. The only even finger that can have a value of 1000_2 is finger 4. A 1 in the fourth position to the left identifies a whorl on finger 4.

In the above example, the numerator is 10101_2, and $10101_2 - 1 = 10100_2$. The 1 in the fifth position to the left tells you there is a whorl on finger 2 (the right index finger), and the 1 in the third position to the left identifies a whorl on finger 6 (left thumb). The 0s in the remaining positions tell you that there is no whorl on fingers 4, 8, and 10. The 1s in the denominator identify the location of whorls on the odd-numbered fingers in a similar way. In the above example the denominator is 11_2, and $11_2 - 1 = 10_2$. The 1 in the second position to the left identifies a whorl on finger 7. The 0 on the right and the implied 0s on the left indicate that there are no whorls on fingers 1, 3, 5, and 9.

Another example will help clarify why the "added-on 1" needs to be subtracted before identification of whorls can take place. The binary primary classification is

$$\frac{1010_2}{10_2}$$

To determine the location of whorls on the even fingers, you would first subtract the added-on 1; $1010_2 - 1 = 1001_2$. The 1 in the far left position indicates a whorl on finger 4, and the 1 in the far right position indicates a whorl on finger 10. To determine the location of whorls on the odd fingers, subtract the added-on 1; $10_2 - 1 = 1_2$, indicating a whorl on finger 9.

On Student Sheet 4.3, students gain more practice with this binary system as they calculate the binary primary classification for all members in their groups.

On Student Sheet 4.4, students locate the whorls from the binary primary classifications of members in another group. Students discover that working with binary classifications (base 2) is easier than working with the primary classifications in base 10. At this point, you should focus on the similarities of the system structures, that is the structure of base 2 compared to the structure of base 10. One important aspect to stress is the role of place value.

The Writing Link "Binary World" is referred to in the Discussion Questions.

Presenting the Activity

Ten to Two. Review with the class the pattern that facilitates the under-standing of the definition that $2^0=1$. Elicit from the class that

$$2 = 2^1$$
$$4 = 2^2$$
$$8 = 2^3$$
$$16 = 2^4$$
$$32 = 2^5$$

Elicit from the class what the above pattern is. Make sure they understand that as the standard form increases by a factor of 2, the exponent increases by 1. Now start with $32 = 2^5$ and decrease the exponent by 1,

$$16 = 2^4$$
$$8 = 2^3$$
$$4 = 2^2$$
$$2 = 2^1$$

Elicit what the pattern is. Students will see that dividing the standard form by 2 is equivalent to decreasing the exponent by 1. Help students find the unknown in the following:

$$1 = 2^?$$

Divide students into small working groups. Hand out Student Sheet 4.1, and have the groups discuss the similarities and differences between base 10 and base 2. Using a transparency of Student Sheet 4.1, orchestrate a dis-cussion of their findings. Have students complete Student Sheet 4.1, and as a class, discuss the binary system.

Binary Classification. Hand out Student Sheet 4.2 and, if necessary, each student's Student Sheet 3.2. Using Transparency Master 4.6, discuss the translation of the whorl values to binary numbers. Have students calculate their binary primary classification index. Hand out Student Sheet 4.3 and have students calculate the binary primary classification of every member of their group, or for variety, they can calculate the binary primary classifi-cation of every member of some other group.

More Finger Math. Hand out Student Sheet 4.4 and explain that this is similar to the decoding task they did with the primary classification indexes in base 10. Now they are to decode the binary primary classification indices in base 2 to determine the location of whorls. They will discover that the location is almost immediate once they subtract the 1, the positions (place value positions) of the 1s in the numerator will identify the even fingers that have whorls, and the position of the 1s in the denominator will identify the odd fingers that have whorls. However, they must first remember to subtract the 1! To ensure that everyone in the class discovers how efficient it is to use the binary system, have the groups share their techniques.

Binary Systems. Hand out Student Sheet 4.5. Explain to the groups they are to discuss and then put in writing why the Henry Primary Classification System is a binary system whether one uses base 10 or base 2 numerals. They are to give examples of coding and decoding the systems to support their positions. Some students might have already realized this in the discussion of the filing procedures. At each step in the procedure, the decision is made on the basis of two possible outcomes: the presence of a whorl or the absence of a whorl. This is the critical issue.

In addition, they are to discuss and describe what base system would be needed for a classification index that assigned numerical values to all three pattern types—whorls, loops, and arches. Again, they should give examples to support their position.

Discussion Questions

1. Compare and contrast the primary classification systems using decimal versus binary numbers.

2. Read the Writing Link "Binary World." As directed, list other real-world phenomena that are examples of a binary number system. Explain your thinking on each one.

3. How many characteristics would one need to have a base 10 classification system? Explain your thinking.

Assessment Questions

1. Compare and contrast $2^1_2 + 2^2_2 + 2^3_2$ with $10^1 + 10^2 + 10^3$.

2. Develop a primary classification system that gives points for whorls, arches, and loops.

3. Write a brief paper comparing and contrasting a base 2 and a base 10 number system. Use sufficient examples to enable a parent to follow your reasoning.

Binary World

You have learned about fingerprint classification as a binary number system. Binary means there are two options. In the case of fingerprint classification, the options are "whorl" or "no whorl." What other examples of binary number systems can you think of? Computers are one example. Their language consists of 1s and 0s.

Make a list of other binary number systems. Think about real-world phenomena. Think about examples in nature. Explain your thinking on each item in your list.

Ten to Two

Number Systems		
Decimal (Base 10)		Binary (Base 2)
$10^0 = 1$		$1 = 2^0 = 1_2$
$10^1 = 10$		$2 = 2^1 = 10_2$
$10^2 = 100$		$4 = 2^2 = 100_2$
$10^3 = 1000$		$8 = 2^3 = 1000_2$
$10^4 = 10000$		$16 = 2^4 = 10000_2$

Write the following numbers as sums of powers of 2 and then in base 2.

Base 10	Sums of Powers of 2	Base 2
1	2^0	1_2
2	2^1	10_2
3	$2^1 + 2^0$	11_2
4		
5		
6		
7		
8		
9		
10		
11		
12		
13		
14		
15		
16		

Base 10	Sums of Powers of 2	Base 2
17		
18		
19		
20		
21		
22		
23		
24		
25		
26		
27		
28		
29		
30		
31		
32		

Ten to Two

Do the following problems in both the decimal system and the binary system.

Decimal System	Binary System

1. 16 + 8 = $10000_2 + 1000_2 =$

2. 32 + 4 =

3. 16 + 2 =

4. 32 + 16 + 8 + 1 =

5. 32 + 16 + 4 + 2 =

6. 32 + 16 + 8 + 4 + 2 + 1 =

7. 31 − 1 =

8. 16 − 2 =

9. 13 − 3 =

10. 18 − 1 =

Binary Primary

1. Below is the Henry Primary Classification System given in decimal form for each hand and then for the even versus the odd fingers. Translate the whorl values to binary and record them in the binary primary classification form at the bottom of the page.

Henry Primary Classification (Decimal—Right versus Left Hand)

	1 Thumb	2 Index	3 Middle	4 Ring	5 Little
Right Hand	16	16	8	8	4

	6 Thumb	7 Index	8 Middle	9 Ring	10 Little
Left Hand	4	2	2	1	1

Henry Primary Classification (Decimal—Even versus Odd Fingers)

	2 Index	4 Ring	6 Thumb	8 Middle	10 Little
Even Fingers	16	8	4	2	1

	1 Thumb	3 Middle	5 Little	7 Index	9 Ring
Odd Fingers	16	8	4	2	1

Binary Primary Classification

	2 Index	4 Ring	6 Thumb	8 Middle	10 Little
Even Fingers					

	1 Thumb	3 Middle	5 Little	7 Index	9 Ring
Odd Fingers					

2. Using your Student Sheet 3.2, calculate the binary primary classification for your fingers.

Binary Primary Classification

Calculate the binary primary classification for the other members in your group.

1. Name _____   Primary Classification _____

	2 Index	4 Ring	6 Thumb	8 Middle	10 Little
Even Fingers	10000_2	1000_2	100_2	10_2	1_2

	1 Thumb	3 Middle	5 Little	7 Index	9 Ring
Odd Fingers	10000_2	1000_2	100_2	10_2	1_2

2. Name _____   Primary Classification _____

	2 Index	4 Ring	6 Thumb	8 Middle	10 Little
Even Fingers	10000_2	1000_2	100_2	10_2	1_2

	1 Thumb	3 Middle	5 Little	7 Index	9 Ring
Odd Fingers	10000_2	1000_2	100_2	10_2	1_2

3. Name _____   Primary Classification _____

	2 Index	4 Ring	6 Thumb	8 Middle	10 Little
Even Fingers	10000_2	1000_2	100_2	10_2	1_2

	1 Thumb	3 Middle	5 Little	7 Index	9 Ring
Odd Fingers	10000_2	1000_2	100_2	10_2	1_2

More Finger Math

	2 Index	4 Ring	6 Thumb	8 Middle	10 Little
Even Fingers	10000_2	1000_2	100_2	10_2	1_2

	1 Thumb	3 Middle	5 Little	7 Index	9 Ring
Odd Fingers	10000_2	1000_2	100_2	10_2	1_2

1. In the table below, fill in the name and binary primary classification for each member in your group. Do not fill in the whorl location data.

2. Exchange papers with another group.

3. As a group, determine the whorl locations for each primary classification listed below. You might want to review the procedure you used on Student Sheet 3.4.

4. When both your group and the group with which you exchanged papers have finished, again exchange papers and check each other's work.

5. As a group, be prepared to explain your decoding system and why it works. Be prepared to compare and contrast the decimal primary classification and the binary primary classification systems.

My Group

Name	Primary Classification	Whorl Locations

Binary Systems

1. Explain in writing why the Henry Primary Classification Fingerprint System is a binary system whether one uses base 10 or base 2 numerals. Use examples of encoding and decoding primary classifications to support your argument.

2. Explain what type of system would be needed to incorporate information on all three types of fingerprint patterns—whorls, loops, and arches.

Ten to Two

Number Systems	
Decimal (Base 10)	Binary (Base 2)
$10^0 = 1$	$1 = 2^0 = 1_2$
$10^1 = 10$	$2 = 2^1 = 10_2$
$10^2 = 100$	$4 = 2^2 = 100_2$
$10^3 = 1000$	$8 = 2^3 = 1000_2$
$10^4 = 10000$	$16 = 2^4 = 10000_2$

Henry Primary Classification (Decimal—Right versus Left Hand)

	1 Thumb	2 Index	3 Middle	4 Ring	5 Little
Right Hand	16	16	8	8	4

	6 Thumb	7 Index	8 Middle	9 Ring	10 Little
Left Hand	4	2	2	1	1

Henry Primary Classification (Decimal—Even versus Odd Fingers)

	2 Index	4 Ring	6 Thumb	8 Middle	10 Little
Even Fingers	16	8	4	2	1

	1 Thumb	3 Middle	5 Little	7 Index	9 Ring
Odd Fingers	16	8	4	2	1

Binary Primary Classification

	2 Index	4 Ring	6 Thumb	8 Middle	10 Little
Even Fingers					

	1 Thumb	3 Middle	5 Little	7 Index	9 Ring
Odd Fingers					

ACTIVITY
5

LOOPS, ARCHES, AND WHORLS

Overview

Students determine the frequencies of each type of fingerprint pattern for the class as a whole and graphically display the data. In addition, they create plots illustrating the relation between fingerprint pattern and gender as well as the relation between fingerprint pattern and specific fingers.

Time. Two 40- to 50-minute periods.

Purpose. Students gain much experience in data collection, analysis, and graphic representation as they discover that the majority of fingerprints are loops while arches appear the least frequently. They also discover that the frequency of whorls is not the same for each finger, and that it differs with gender.

Materials. *For the teacher:*

◆ Transparencies of Student Sheets 5.1, 5.3, and 5.4

For each student:

◆ Student Sheets 5.1–5.5
◆ Completed Student Sheet 3.2

Getting Ready

1. Duplicate Student Sheets 5.1–5.5.
2. Prepare transparencies of Student Sheets 5.1, 5.3, and 5.4.
3. Locate each student's completed Student Sheet 3.2 (unless students already have them from Activity 3).

Background Information

In this activity, students collect the fingerprint patterns as a function of finger and gender for every student in the class. They then analyze and graph the data as a function of gender and as a function of finger. Students complete this activity by summarizing all the findings and hypothesizing how it might be used by a law enforcement agency. This activity could easily be extended; there are many interesting questions students could investigate by doing further analyses of the class data. (The question of whether or not pattern types are inherited forms the basis of the Family Activity.) The Interest Link "Frequency of Fingerprint Patterns" gives information on the percentages of people with loops, whorls, and arches on their fingerprint patterns.

If you are doing this activity with more than one class, consider grouping the data from all classes to form an even larger sample size. While the differences in frequencies of pattern types will be in evidence in small sample sizes, the posited differences as function of gender, ethnology, and finger position would be more reliably addressed with a larger sample size.

On Student Sheet 5.1, students record the name, gender, and fingerprint pattern type of all ten fingers for each student in the class. Then on Student Sheet 5.2, they tally the numbers of loops, arches, and whorls recorded on Student Sheet 5.1.

On Student Sheets 5.1 and 5.2, students compare the frequencies of patterns by gender and by finger number on bar graphs. Students are then asked to write a summary of their findings on Student Sheet 5.5.

Now that students are more familiar with fingerprint patterns, they may be able to think of creative ways to use fingerprinting. In the Writing Link "Other Uses for Fingerprinting," students may describe their original ideas. This Writing Link may be used at any time during the activity.

Presenting the Activity

Classy Patterns. Divide the class into small working groups. Hand out or have each student locate Student Sheet 3.2 on which they recorded their fingerprint pattern types. Hand out Student Sheet 5.1. Display a transparency of Student Sheet 5.1 and have each student record on the transparency his or her name, gender, and fingerprint pattern types for each finger. Have them record the information from the overhead on their own data sheets. Caution students to record the data onto their student sheets in exactly the same order as they appear on the transparency. This will simplify any checking of the data should discrepancies occur.

The LAW. When all students have recorded their data on the transparency and their own sheets, hand out Student Sheet 5.2. Using the data on Student Sheet 5.1, students are to tabulate the number of loops, arches, and whorls for each student and to record the summary data on Student Sheet 5.2. After students have calculated the totals, discuss their findings. Read or hand out copies of the Interest Link "Frequency of Fingerprint Patterns." If students raise questions that are not addressed in the Interest Link, suggest they research the issue and report back to the class.

Women and the LAW. Hand out Student Sheet 5.3. Using the data on Student Sheet 5.2, students are to tabulate the numbers of loops, arches, and whorls for females, for males, and for the total as a check. Have them check each other's work within their groups and come to consensus as to the correctness of the data. Encourage variety if some members prefer to present the data in differing displays, however, after discussion the group may prepare like graphs. Once the data are displayed, discuss students' findings. Elicit possible explanations for the findings and questions for further study.

The Finger of the LAW. Hand out Student Sheet 5.4. Using the data on Student Sheet 5.2, students are to tabulate the number of loops, arches, and whorls for each finger and for the total as a check. Have them check each other's work within their groups and come to consensus as to the correctness of the data. The group can prepare like or individually-differing graphs. This could be done as homework. In either case, allow time for discussion of the findings and share some of the results of research based on the relation of pattern type to specific finger. Again, elicit topics for further research.

LAW Summary. Hand out Student Sheet 5.5. The groups should discuss their findings regarding the distribution of loops, arches, and whorls. If time permits, the groups could compose statements regarding their hypotheses on how this type of information might be used by a law enforcement agency, or this could be assigned as a homework project for each student to work on individually.

Discussion Questions

1. There appear to be differences in the occurrence of loops, arches, and whorls as a function of gender. Why do you think this might be?

2. List other variables that might influence the distribution of fingerprint patterns. Explain why you think there would be such an influence.

3. It is hypothesized that types of fingerprint patterns are inherited. Do you think this is so?

Assessment Questions

1. It is hypothesized that the frequency of the types of fingerprint patterns differ as a function of ethnic background. Collect the necessary data to add to the information on Student Sheet 5.1. Analyze the data as a function of ethnic differences, graph the results, and write a brief news report on your findings.

2. It is hypothesized that there is a "bilateralism" in fingerprint distribution, that is, the same fingers on both hands tend to have the same type of pattern. The index fingers tend to have the same type of pattern, and the thumbs tend to have the same type of pattern, and so on. Discuss this concept with your group, and design a plan to investigate such an hypothesis. Outline your investigative plan.

3. As a group, make an hypothesis regarding the distribution of types of fingerprint patterns. Design a plan to test the hypothesis. Collect and analyze the data. Write a brief summary of your findings, including a graph of the results.

Frequency of Fingerprint Patterns

Look at your fingertips. How many whorls do you have? How many whorls do you think your friends have on their fingers? Researchers have often wondered which are more common—loops, arches, or whorls.

One of the first studies on the distribution of types of fingerprint patterns came from a Scotland Yard report. The study of 5,000 British men and women of different ethnic backgrounds showed that 70 percent of the patterns were loops, 25 percent were whorls, and only 5 percent were arches. Current accepted frequencies for the general population in the United States are approximately 65 percent loops, 30 percent whorls, and 5 percent arches.

Some research also shows that fingerprint patterns tend to vary based on a person's ethnicity and gender. However, other research says the opposite, so there are still unanswered questions.

There are more questions about whether fingerprint patterns appear with the same frequency on each hand. In the Scotland Yard report, there were more loops on the left hand (72 percent) than on the right hand (67 percent) and more whorls on the right hand (29 percent) than on the left (22 percent). The distribution of arches was about the same on both hands—4 percent on the right hand and 5 percent on the left hand. There were also questions about the frequency of types on each finger. There were many more whorls on both thumbs than on any other finger, and the little fingers on both hands displayed the greatest number of loops.

This brings up another question. Do the same fingers on each hand tend to have the same pattern? That is, do the index fingers both have the same type of pattern? The data suggest this might be true. What does your research show about the frequency of fingerprint types?

Other Uses for Fingerprinting

In ancient times, fingerprints were sometimes used as personal "seals" on important documents. In some cultures, they even took the place of a handwritten signature. Today, fingerprinting is most often linked to criminal investigations. But what other uses are there for this remarkably unique print—a marking so unique that the possibility of two people having identical prints is estimated to be only once in 4,660,377 centuries?

You know some practical uses already. Children are fingerprinted to help identify them in case they are reported missing. Some banks, military bases, and government offices check employee's fingerprints before they can enter restricted areas. Computers have been created that read fingerprints in a matter of seconds, and if the computer recognizes the fingerprint, it allows the user to enter doors or computer files.

Think of other ways fingerprinting can be used in our society. Be creative. Also, you may do research to discover more about the uses of fingerprints in areas other than criminal investigations. For example, research how some scientists believe certain fingerprint patterns show abnormalities in a person's chromosomes (the genetic code of a person). Can the patterns reveal if a person will get Alzheimer's disease, cancer, or diabetes?

Write a short essay on your ideas for different uses of fingerprinting.

Classy Patterns

Record the pattern type on each finger for each student in your class. Use *L* for loop, *A* for arch, and *W* for whorl.

Name	Gender	Finger									
		1	2	3	4	5	6	7	8	9	10

The LAW

From your class data, calculate the number of loops, arches, and whorls (LAW) for each student in your class.

Name	Gender	Loops	Arches	Whorls
TOTAL				

Women and the LAW

Calculate the number of loops, arches, and whorls for all the females in your class and for all the males.

Gender	Loops	Arches	Whorls
Females			
Males			
TOTAL			

Make a bar graph illustrating the relation between loops, arches, and whorls and gender.

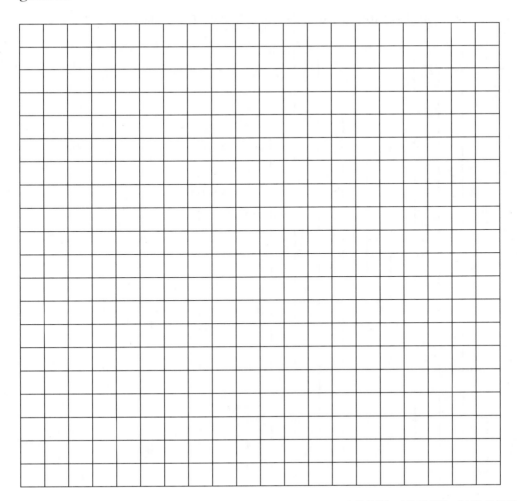

The Finger of the LAW

Calculate the number of loops, arches, and whorls on each finger for all students in your class.

Class LAW	Finger									
	1	2	3	4	5	6	7	8	9	10
Loops										
Arches										
Whorls										
TOTAL										

Make a bar graph illustrating the relation between fingerprint pattern and finger.

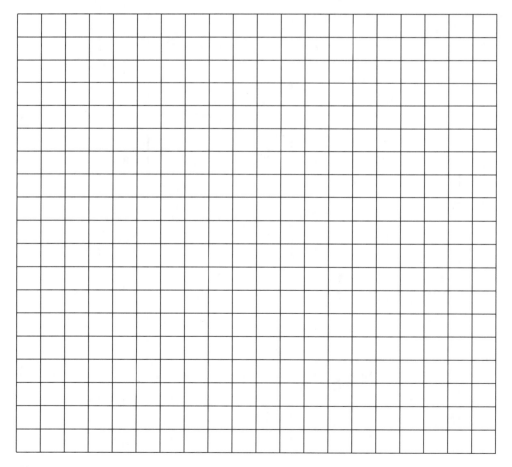

LAW Summary

Write a brief statement describing your findings regarding the frequency of LAW (loops, arches, and whorls) by gender and by finger. Hypothesize how these findings might be used by the law (police).

ACTIVITY
6

THE NATIONAL CRIME INFORMATION CENTER

Overview

Students learn how the National Crime Information Center (NCIC) classifies and stores fingerprint classifications (FPCs) in its computer files. Students calculate their codes and relate them to their primary classifications.

Time. Two 40- to 50-minute periods.

Purpose. Students investigate the current computer method of filing fingerprint information. They learn that it contains the primary classification information along with further data on each fingerprint.

Materials. *For the teacher:*

◆ Transparency Master 6.5

◆ A transparency of Student Sheet 6.1

◆ A transparency of ridge-count diagram in Background Information (optional)

For each student:

◆ Student Sheets 6.1–6.4

◆ Completed Student Sheet 1.2

◆ Magnifying glass

Getting Ready

1. Duplicate Student Sheets 6.1–6.4.

2. Prepare a transparency of Student Sheet 6.1.

3. Prepare Transparency Master 6.5.

4. Locate magnifying glasses.

5. Locate each student's completed Student Sheet 1.2 (unless students already have them from Activity 1).

6. Prepare a transparency of the page in the Background Information that shows "Ridge Counts on Two Loops" (optional).

Background Information

The National Crime Information Center (NCIC) is a computerized system established to provide information to federal, state, and local law enforcement agencies. It contains numerous types of files, one of which is the Fingerprint Classification (FPC) file. Another well-known file maintained by the NCIC is the "wanted person" file. The information is stored on a computer and transmitted to agencies in the computer network via the information highway—by communication lines, modems, and terminals.

This activity is time consuming, but most students find it quite exciting to "work for the FBI." If time is a factor, this activity is optional.

The FPC is stored in the computer as a twenty-digit alpha-numeric field (it contains both letters and numbers). Each finger is coded with a two-digit code. The information is stored left to right starting with the code of finger 1 through the code of finger 10. The two-digit code reveals detailed information on the pattern that exists on the finger. It is not a positive identifier, but it greatly reduces the sample. A more careful examination is needed to provide a positive match.

The FPC contains information that is new to our investigation of fingerprint patterns. Loops and whorls are surrounded by *type lines,* which are defined as the two innermost ridges that run parallel to each other near the outside of the print and then diverge in opposite directions to surround the print area. The *delta* is the nearest point in front of the innermost divergence of the type lines. It was named after the Greek letter delta, the symbol of which is a triangle. The Greeks called the triangular-shaped sand deposit that accumulated at the mouth of a river a *delta.* The diagram below highlights the type lines and deltas in a loop. The heavy lines A–A and B–B are type lines, and the delta is at point D.

The FPC differentiates between two types of loops—radial loops and ulnar loops. The wrist has two bones: the radius, the bone on the inside of the wrist closer to the thumb; and the ulna, the bone on the outer side of

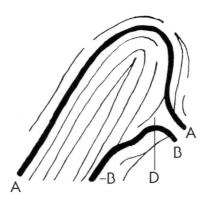

the wrist closer to the little finger. If a loop originates, curves, and exits from the thumb side of the finger, it is a radial loop. If it originates, curves, and exits from the outer side of the wrist, it is an ulnar loop. All loops have one delta. Transparency Master 6.5 gives examples of both types of loops. Note that an ulnar loop on the left hand (a left ulnar loop) has the same orientation as a radial loop on the right hand (a right radial loop), as does a right ulnar loop and a left radial loop.

The FPC differentiates between two types of arches: plain arches and tented arches. In plain arches, all the ridges enter from one side of the finger and exit from the other. In tented arches, the middle ridge might end in the center of the print; it might not continue to the other side. However, it does not curve back, as in a loop, it just ends. Arches have no deltas. See Transparency Master 6.5 for examples of both types of arches.

The FPC differentiates four categories of whorls, all having at least two deltas. Both plain whorls and central loop whorls have a central core that looks like a circle or a spiral with at least one other ridge that encircles it. The differentiating characteristic involves an imaginary line between the two deltas. If this imaginary line crosses one of the ridges that encircles the central core, it is a plain whorl. If this imaginary line, however, does not cross one of these encircling ridges, the whorl is labeled a central loop whorl.

The third category of whorls is easily recognizable by its name—the double loop whorl. It consists of two opposing spirals. The fourth and last category, the accidental whorl, consists of prints that do not conform to any given definition. Any combination of patterns or any pattern that cannot clearly be put in one of the above categories is labeled accidental. Transparency Master 6.5 gives examples of all four types of whorls.

The FPC contains information on the ridge count for any loop. The ridge count is the number of ridges between the most central ridge (the core) and the ridge that emanates from the delta. If the central ridge ends, it is considered the core. If the central ridge curves back on itself, the side of this ridge farthest from the delta is considered the core. The diagram below gives two examples of loops and their ridge counts.

The FPC contains one last piece of new information, whorl tracing, which is a measure of the relative position of the two deltas within a whorl. To determine the whorl tracing, identify the lowest ridge emanating from the left delta—the left type line—and trace it until it either meets, passes above, or passes below the right delta. If the left type line passes above the right delta by three or more ridges, the tracing is called an *inner tracing*. If the left type line passes within two ridges of the right delta, it is called a *meeting tracing*. If the left type line goes below the right delta by three or more ridges, it is called on *outer tracing*. The second page of Student Sheet 6.2 gives examples of all three types of tracings.

You are now ready to work for the FBI! The NCIC FPC is given on Student Sheet 6.3. Note that in order to differentiate a radial loop from an ulnar loop, the code adds 50 to the ridge count of a radial loop. The rest of the code is straightforward. The code *scarred* is used only as a last resort, when the print is so scarred or mutilated that the pattern cannot be clearly determined.

The Career Link "FBI Agents," the Technology Link "Fingerprint Locks," and the Interest Link "Other Methods of 'Printing'" can be used at any time during this activity to spark interest.

Ridge Count on Two Loops

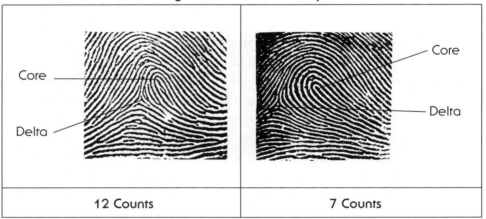

12 Counts	7 Counts

Presenting the Activity

Cores, Deltas, and Ridges. Divide students into small working groups. Using the Background Information as reference, discuss with the class what the Fingerprint Classification (FPC) file is. Explain the terms *delta* and *core*. Discuss the way a ridge count is taken, depending on whether the core ridge ends or folds back upon itself. You may want to use a transparency of the diagram "Ridge Count on Two Loops" in the Background Information for this discussion.

Hand out Student Sheet 6.1 and, if necessary, each student's completed Student Sheet 1.2 (their sets of fingerprints). Also hand out magnifying glasses.

After the groups have had a few minutes to study and discuss the fingerprint on Student Sheet 6.1, display a transparency of it. Elicit from students the location of the core, the delta, and the ridge count. Have students take a ridge count on one of their own loops and then discuss the process in their groups to make sure everyone fully understands it. Have them do a ridge count on a loop from someone else in their group.

Pattern Differentiation. Have each student examine one of their loops. Ask them to describe the positioning of the loop on their finger. It will quickly come out that some loops open outward, toward the little finger, and others open inward, toward the thumb. Ask students if they have studied the skeleton. Many will have done so. Have them recall the names of the wrist bones. Elicit whether anyone has a mnemonic device for remembering which is which. Point out that the loops are named by the direction they open. Those opening toward the thumb (toward the radius) are called *radial* loops, and those opening toward the little finger (toward the ulna) are called *ulnar* loops. Display Transparency Master 6.5, and as a class, examine the two types of loops. They will notice that a left ulnar and a right radial loop look alike. Elicit an explanation.

Continue displaying Transparency Master 6.5. Hand out Student Sheet 6.2 and have the groups examine the various types of loops, arches, and whorls. As questions come up, use the transparency and the information on Student Sheet 6.2 to clarify the differentiations.

When the groups appear to understand the differentiations, orchestrate a class discussion focused on whorl tracing. First identify the two deltas, then identify the type line emanating from the left delta. Have students trace the type line to determine if it goes above, goes below, or meets the right delta.

NCIC FPC. Inform students they are now ready to "work for the FBI," and hand out Student Sheet 6.3. Have students investigate the code within their groups. Ask why they think 50 is added to the radial loop ridge counts. Have them code the fingerprints on Student Sheet 6.2. As the groups are ready, hand out Student Sheet 6.4, and have them determine the fingerprint patterns for the given FPC to determine their own FPCs.

Discussion Questions

1. Why is 50 added to the ridge count of radial loops?

2. Which are the most difficult patterns to differentiate? Explain.

3. List what types of files might be kept by the NCIC.

4. What do you think the probability is of having identical codes? How would you calculate the probability?

Assessment Questions

1. As a group project, collect the data you need to add to Student Sheet 5.1 in order to determine if the frequency of one of the following differ:

   a. the two types of loops

   b. the two types of arches

   c. the four types of whorls

2. Take fingerprints from family members and determine their FPCs.

3. Exchange codes with a member of another group. Decode their code, and write a descriptive statement of all the fingerprint patterns in language a friend not in the class could understand.

FBI Agents

Someone working on a top-secret military plane may be selling blueprints to spies from another country. The President of the United States has received a note threatening assassination. A cruise ship has been hijacked by terrorists off the coast of Puerto Rico. What do each of these crimes have in common? They would all be handled by special agents for the FBI.

FBI agents are responsible for investigating federal crimes. In their work, agents deal with organized crime, kidnappings, bombings, interstate thefts, drug smugglers, violations of toxic waste dumping, and many other crimes. The FBI also collects information, called *intelligence,* about organizations or people it believes may threaten national security.

In the movies, special agents seem to live a life of continual action and excitement. In reality, FBI agents spend a lot of time researching, asking questions, collecting evidence, and filing reports. But FBI agents will at times face danger as they attempt to solve cases.

In order to become one of the approximately 9,400 special agents of the FBI, you first need to be a United States citizen between 23 and 35 years of age and be in excellent physical shape. You must also have a college degree in accounting, law, language, science, or engineering. You may instead have a degree in another field plus three years of work experience. Many agents also have graduate degrees.

Your next step is to get into the FBI National Academy. At the academy, you go through a 15-week training program that teaches you investigative methods, how to collect evidence, criminal law, self-defense, and how to use firearms. You will take classes on fingerprinting, interviewing procedures, and how to detect forged documents. You will also take a strenuous physical education program.

At the end of the 15 weeks, you are officially presented your FBI badge and given your assignment in one of the 75 FBI offices in the United States and around the world.

Fingerprint Locks

Suppose you have invented an amazing liquid that can make plants grow to twice their normal size. Another company has heard rumors about your miracle plant food and will do anything to steal the formula. Security guards at your company have already caught one spy who dressed up to look like one of your lab workers. The president of your company wants you to make sure only you and your team of a hundred scientists are allowed to get into the laboratory.

You decide to install fingerprint analysis locks on the doors. These devices have been around since 1980. Some banks use them to keep unauthorized people out of vaults, several companies have them attached to computer terminals to thwart anyone who tries to get into private computer files, and a few can even be found protecting the doors to deluxe wine cellars.

The device is a small, plastic box that goes by the door to the lab. To enter the lab, you place your finger on the reader window of the box three times. A camera in the box takes pictures of your fingerprint. Then a computer combines the pictures into a two-dimensional image and compares it to fingerprint images stored in the software library. There are only 101 fingerprints in the library (yours and those of your workers). If the computer finds a match, the door opens. The whole process takes about three seconds.

Several spies try to break into the lab, but the computer can tell whether the finger on the reader window belongs to someone who is allowed to enter. No matter what other tricks they have up their sleeves, the spies can not change their fingerprints.

Your formula remains a secret. The incredible plant food becomes a great success, much to the dismay of your rival company.

Other Methods of "Printing"

The patterns of ridges on your fingers are not the only unique prints you have. Your feet, toes, palms, voice, and even the DNA in your cells can provide unmistakable prints that identify you as you.

Just as no two people's fingerprints are alike, no two people have the same footprints. Hospitals sometimes make footprints of infants' feet soon after they are born. This helps prevent accidental "baby switches."

Palm prints are also unique for every individual. They are treated like fingerprints. Sometimes, detectives can find palm prints even if the criminal was wearing gloves. Gloves slip open, and the culprit may unknowingly press a print onto a windowsill or other surface.

Every person's voice makes its own combination of sound waves. By running a tape recording of the voice through a sound spectrograph, the voice can be turned into a "print" that shows its specific loudness, pitch, and quality. These voiceprints can identify individuals, for example, someone who has been recorded making obscene phone calls. However, some scientists believe voiceprints are not accurate enough to use in court since they are difficult to interpret.

Another recent development is DNA fingerprinting. DNA is the genetic material in every cell of every person that makes one unique. If investigators find blood, hair, skin, saliva, or other traces of a person's presence at the scene of a crime, these specimens can be brought to a laboratory. Scientists then sort the DNA into a genetic pattern—a pattern that no two people share, not even identical twins.

What types of "prints" will criminalists be looking for in the future? As DNA fingerprinting becomes more accurate and less expensive, it may be the "fingerprint dusting" of tomorrow. Or, scientists may find other ways to make "prints" of the uniqueness of every person.

Cores, Deltas, and Ridges

1. Every loop has a core, one delta, and ridges. Examine the loop below. Do the following:
   a. Find the *core*—the center ridge.
   b. Find the *delta*—that point on a ridge at or in front of and nearest the divergence of the type lines.
   c. Determine the *ridge count*—the number of ridges between the core and the ridge that forms the delta.

2. Using a magnifying glass, examine one of your fingerprints that is a loop. Locate its core, its delta, and determine the ridge count.

Finger Number	Ridge Count

3. When you have finished, trade fingerprints with a member of your group. Determine the new fingerprint's ridge count.

Name of Group Member	Finger Number	Ridge Count

4. Check each other's work.

Pattern Differentiation

The National Crime Information Center (NCIC) Fingerprint Classification (FPC) files record specific information for each type of pattern—loops, arches, and whorls. In fact, they differentiate among different forms of each of these types of patterns. The following chart gives all the different types of patterns. Work with your group to make sure everyone knows the differences between the various subpatterns.

Fingerprint Pattern Differentiation

Pattern	Examples			
Loop	Left Ulnar	Left Radial	Right Radial	Right Ulnar
Arch	Plain	Plain	Tented	Tented
Whorl	Plain	Central	Double	Accidental

Loops:

There are two types of loops, and both types always have one delta.

Radial loops—The ridges appear to come from and return to the radial bone which is close to the thumb.

Ulnar loops—The ridges appear to come from and return to the ulna which is close to the little finger.

Arches:

There are two types of arches, and neither type has a delta.

Plain arches—All the ridges come in from one side and go out the other.

Tented arches—The middle ridges will not go from one side to the other—they stop in the center.

Pattern Differentiation

Whorls:

There are four types of whorls, and all four types have two or more deltas.

Plain whorls—The central core looks like a coil or a spiral. It has at least one ridge that encircles the core. An imaginary line drawn between the two deltas would cross one of the ridges that encircle the core.

Central loop pocket—The central core loop looks like a plain whorl, however, if you were to draw an imaginary line between the two deltas, the line would not cross any of the ridges that encircle the core.

Double loop—There are clearly two opposing loops.

Accidental—This classification is used for whorls that are combinations of patterns or do not conform to the definitions above.

The NCIC FPC files also record the type of whorl *tracing* for each whorl.

Whorl Tracing

Whorl			
Whorl Tracing	Inner Tracing (Above)	Meeting Tracing	Outer Tracing (Below)

The lowest ridge coming out from the left delta, called the *left type line,* is traced until it reaches the right delta. The type line will relate to the right delta in one of three ways:

1. It will pass above the right delta by three or more ridges. This is called *inner tracing.*
2. It will pass within two ridges of the right delta. This is called a *meeting tracing.*
3. It will go below the right delta by three or more ridges. This is called an *outer tracing.*

You are now ready to work with the FBI. Proceed to Student Sheet 6.3.

NCIC FPC

The National Crime Information Center (NCIC) maintains a computer bank of information for use by law enforcement agencies at all levels. It is maintained by the FBI, and information is available to all local, state, and federal law enforcement agencies in the criminal justice system.

The NCIC maintains a fingerprint database, and the information is stored in the NCIC Fingerprint Classification (FPC) form, which is different from the primary classification index. Fingerprint files today contain both classifications.

In the FPC file, each finger is given a two-digit code identifying the pattern type.

Pattern Type	Pattern Subgroup	Whorl Tracing	NCIC FPC Code
Loop	Radial	—	ridge count + 50
Loop	Ulnar	—	ridge count
Arch	Plain	—	AA
Arch	Tented	—	TT
Whorl	Plain	Inner	PI
Whorl	Plain	Meeting	PM
Whorl	Plain	Outer	PO
Whorl	Central	Inner	CI
Whorl	Central	Meeting	CM
Whorl	Central	Outer	CO
Whorl	Double	Inner	DI
Whorl	Double	Meeting	DM
Whorl	Double	Outer	DO
Whorl	Accidental	Inner	XI
Whorl	Accidental	Meeting	XM
Whorl	Accidental	Outer	XO
Missing	—	—	XX
Scarred	—	—	SR

Determine the FPC for each fingerprint on Student Sheet 6.2. Write them on the back of this sheet.

NCIC FPC and Me

1. The NCIC FPC (Fingerprint Classification) consists of a twenty-digit code made up of ten two-digit codes, one for each of the ten fingers. The code is read from left to right, beginning with the two-digit code for finger 1 and proceeding in order to the two-digit code for finger 10.

Name	Chris Tyler
NCIC FPC	A A 5 7 P I 0 9 T T 0 4 C M D O 0 6 5 5

a. Determine the fingerprint pattern on each of Chris's fingers.

	1 Thumb	2 Index	3 Middle	4 Ring	5 Little
Right Hand	16	16	8	8	4

	6 Thumb	7 Index	8 Middle	9 Ring	10 Little
Left Hand	4	2	2	1	1

b. Calculate Chris's decimal primary classification.

2. Determine your NCIC FPC and complete the NCIC FPC form below. It is sometimes difficult to differentiate the various whorl patterns. Consult with your group members and refer to Student Sheet 6.2 to help in making any difficult decisions.

Name	
NCIC FPC	

3. When you have finished, exchange papers with a classmate and check each other's work.

Fingerprint Pattern Differentiation

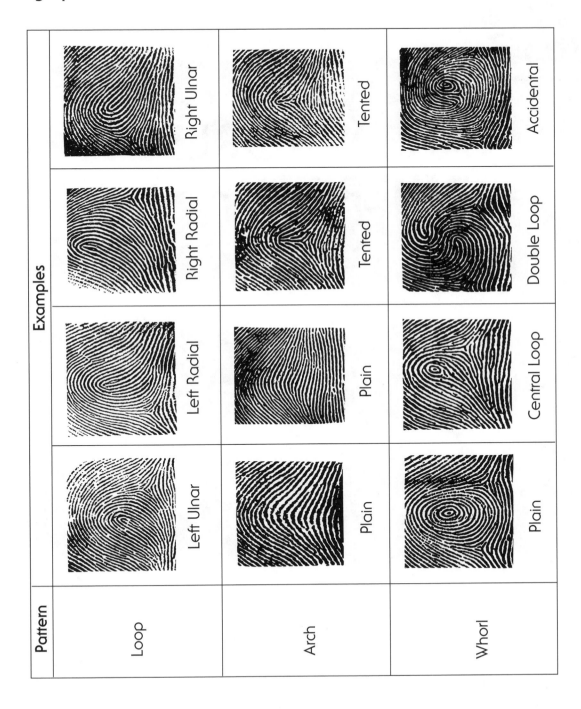

Pattern	Examples			
Loop	Left Ulnar	Left Radial	Right Radial	Right Ulnar
Arch	Plain	Plain	Tented	Tented
Whorl	Plain	Central Loop	Double Loop	Accidental

ARE WHORLS INHERITED?

Overview

Students work with their families to determine the primary fingerprint classification of each family member. Then, as a class, they analyze the number of whorls each person in the family has, graph the data, and decide if there is a relation between the number of whorls the parents have and the number of whorls the offspring have.

Time. At least one hour at home, plus one 40- to 50-minute period in class.

Purpose. Students share with their families what they have learned about fingerprints, data organization, and graphing skills as they investigate the hypothesis that type of fingerprint pattern is inherited.

Materials. *For the teacher:*

◆ A transparency of Family Activity Sheet 3

For each student:

◆ Presenting the Activity pages
◆ Family Activity Sheets 1–3
◆ Completed Student Sheets 1.1–1.2
◆ Magnifying glass

Getting Ready

1. Duplicate Presenting the Activity and Family Activity Sheets 1–3, including extra copies of Family Activity Sheet 1 if necessary.
2. Prepare transparency of Family Activity Sheet 3.
3. Locate magnifying glasses.
4. Locate each student's completed Student Sheets 1.1 and 1.2 (unless students have them already from Activity 1).

Background Information

As discussed previously, there are conflicting data as to whether or not finger pattern types are inherited. Numerous studies have been done throughout the years, and the data are not conclusive. Since it remains an area of study today, students are doing "live" research.

Students and their families determine the pattern type on each finger of all family members. They need to make fingerprints in order to determine the pattern type, but the prints can be discarded once the pattern type is determined. Family Activity Sheet 1 provides space for recording the pattern type. Space is allowed for four sets of prints. Have extra copies available for students who have more than four family members.

Family Activity Sheet 2 provides space to record both the primary and binary classification for each family member. Students can share with their families information on real-world uses of different base number systems.

Family Activity Sheet 3 organizes the data to address the question of whether or not there is a tendency within families to have the same number of whorls. After organizing and graphing the data, the families address the question of whether or not their family data support the hypothesis that whorls are inherited.

The Family Activity would be best done immediately following Activity 5, which focuses on the distribution of fingerprint patterns as functions of different variables. Hand it out at this time along with Student Sheets 1.1 and 1.2 if necessary. Allow sufficient time for the families to schedule an evening when it can be completed.

As mentioned in the Background Information for Activity 5, this question might be more definitively addressed with a larger sample size. Set a date for students to return with their family data. Combine the results for the entire class by having each student graph their data on the same graph, perhaps on a transparency of Family Activity Sheet 3.

Orchestrate a class discussion of this graph. Students will be familiar with the word *correlation,* but they might have differing definitions. Have a dictionary available. Have students in their small groups discuss the meaning of correlation and how to interpret the data. Finish the activity by having some of the groups share their interpretations. Students should be prepared to report the class findings back to their families.

The Interest Link "They Won't Go Away!" and the Writing Link "Write a Mystery" can be used at any time during this activity to spark student interest. The Career Link "Donna West" describes the work of a print supervisor in a police department.

Presenting the Activity

Family Patterns. Discuss with your parents the three types of fingerprint patterns. Have your set of prints on Student Sheet 1.2 to show them, or take prints of some family member and discuss the pattern on each print. Explain that the frequency of each pattern is different. Loops occur with the greatest frequency, somewhere between 60 percent and 70 percent. Whorls are the next most frequent—approximately 30 percent to 35 percent,—and arches are very infrequent, averaging about 5 percent of all fingerprint patterns. Discuss the findings of Activity 5 and how they relate to past studies that show conflicting data regarding the influence of gender and finger position on these frequencies.

Explain the hypothesis that pattern types are inherited. Data suggest offspring tend to have the same frequency of pattern types as their parents. There are however, conflicting data. Some studies support the hypothesis, and others do not. Explain that together you are going to collect data to address this question. Point out that, as a family group, you will analyze your family data, and you will also combine the data for the whole class, analyze it, and report back to them on the findings.

You will need enough copies of Family Activity Sheet 1 to record the fingerprint types for each member of your family. One sheet provides space for four sets of prints, so take as many as you need to do your entire family. You will also need scratch paper, a soft pencil, clear tape, and a magnifying glass. If you want to view the prints as they would appear on a legal form, you will need a piece of clear plastic or mylar.

Assist each member of your family in taking their prints. You might want to have a copy of Student Sheet 1.1 available as you explain the process for taking fingerprints to your family. Assure them that after the pattern is determined and recorded, they can throw away their prints, if they choose. Work as a group on Family Activity Sheet 1 to determine the pattern type of each finger of every family member.

Fingerprint Classifications. Family Activity Sheet 2 shows how to calculate the Henry number. Calculate this in base 10, and then show your family how to translate it to base 2. Discuss with them the ease of using base 2 and how the value in base 2, once you subtract 1, immediately gives the location of each whorl.

Family Whorl Count. Family Activity Sheet 3 asks you to plot the number of whorls in each parent-offspring pair in your family. For instance, if you have three whorls and your mother has two, you would place a dot at the (2,3) position on the graph—the number of whorls the parent has determines the horizontal position, and the number of whorls the offspring has determines the vertical position. This kind of plot is called a *scatter diagram* and it shows whether or not there is a correlation between the parent and offspring data. Discuss what *correlation* means, referring to a dictionary if you choose (a mathematics dictionary if you have access to one), and write a brief statement on whether or not your family data on whorls is correlated.

Take your family data to class on the date requested by your teacher.

They Won't Go Away!

In the 1930s, John Dillinger was a famous outlaw wanted for several murders, bank robberies, and kidnappings. In an attempt to change his fingerprints, Dillinger paid crooked doctors to burn away the skin of his fingertips with acid. Dillinger was pleased with the result—his fingers were smooth. Even if the police caught him, they would not be able to prove he was Dillinger because there would be no prints to compare! One night, Dillinger went to a movie. The police found him and during a shootout, killed Dillinger. Dillinger would never find out that his ploy to hide his identity failed. When police took his fingerprints, the tiny lines had already begun to reform in exactly the same pattern he was born with.

Fingerprints are completely formed before birth. By the time a fetus is five months old, the deepest layer of its skin provides the pattern of ridges that shows up on the outer layer of skin. The ridge patterns never change, even as a person gets older. And the ridge patterns never go away, even if the skin is damaged by cuts, by burns, or, as many criminals will attest, by filing it smooth. Once the damaged area heals, the fingerprint reappears as before.

Write a Mystery

The criminal had worn gloves and successfully fled the scene of the crime without leaving a print anywhere. But the police outsmarted the crook, who had tossed away the rubber gloves before leaving. The police simply turned the gloves inside out and took the fingerprints from the inside.

This is a real case of how fingerprints solved a mystery. Mark Twain was the first author to use fingerprints in a crime story. Twain wrote about a lawyer named "Pudd'nhead Wilson" who used fingerprints to prove the innocence of a pair of twins. This does not seem unusual until you realize the book was written in 1894, several years before fingerprints were used to identify criminals. Twain's story, in fact, helped people accept this strange notion of looking for fingerprints at crime scenes.

Using your own imagination, write a short mystery that centers around fingerprints. Make sure your plot shows how the character or characters use fingerprints to solve a mystery by the end of the story.

Donna West

Working in the identification section of a police department, you could be called upon to take the fingerprints of a murder suspect, or even take the prints of the victim! You might prepare inked and latent prints for analysis, assist the senior identification technicians in processing crime scenes, or enter prints into the Automated Fingerprint Identification System (AFIS).

Donna West is the latent print supervisor for the Seattle Police Department. West says her work is often unpredictable and exciting. She oversees the work of ten latent print examiners, who process and analyze fingerprints. She trains entry-level print examiners and directs crime scene searches to ensure that proper procedures are followed at all times. Sometimes she testifies in court, presenting an analysis of the evidence she and her coworkers have gathered. Her job entails everything from performing chemical analysis of the evidence to writing reports.

West studied criminal justice at Washington State University, receiving a B.S. in Police Science and Administration. She studied many topics critical to her daily work responsibilities—chemistry, biology, social sciences, law, English, and photography.

Family Patterns

Determine the fingerprint pattern for each finger of every member of your family. You do not need to record the print.

Name _____

	Thumb	Index	Middle	Ring	Little
Right Hand					

	Thumb	Index	Middle	Ring	Little
Left Hand					

Name _____

	Thumb	Index	Middle	Ring	Little
Right Hand					

	Thumb	Index	Middle	Ring	Little
Left Hand					

Name _____

	Thumb	Index	Middle	Ring	Little
Right Hand					

	Thumb	Index	Middle	Ring	Little
Left Hand					

Name _____

	Thumb	Index	Middle	Ring	Little
Right Hand					

	Thumb	Index	Middle	Ring	Little
Left Hand					

Fingerprint Classification

	1 Thumb	2 Index	3 Middle	4 Ring	5 Little
Right Hand	16	16	8	8	4

	6 Thumb	7 Index	8 Middle	9 Ring	10 Little
Left Hand	4	2	2	1	1

1. The number in the upper left corner of each box is the finger number. For instance, the thumb on the right hand is called finger number 1.

2. The number in the lower right hand corner of each box is the classification value for a whorl.

3. The primary classification of fingerprints is based on the number and location of whorls. No value is given to arches or loops.

4. Primary classification is given as a fraction, and it is calculated by the following formula:

$$\frac{\text{sum of values for whorls of even-numbered fingers} + 1}{\text{sum of values for whorls of odd-numbered fingers} + 1}$$

5. Calculate the primary and binary classification for each member in your family.

Name and Relation	Number of Whorls	Primary Classification	Binary Classification

Family Whorl Count

1. On how many parents do you have whorl information?

2. On how many sons and daughters do you have whorl information?

3. How many parent-offspring pairs can you make? List them.

4. For each parent-offspring pair, plot the number of whorls the parent has on the horizontal axis and the number of whorls the offspring has on the vertical axis.

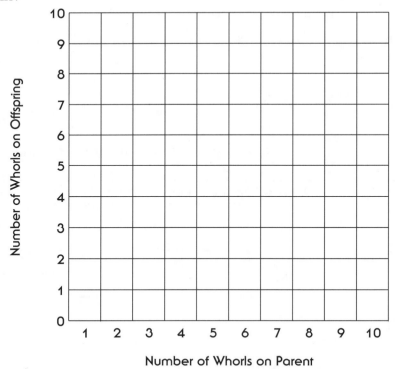

5. Based on your data, do you think whorls are inherited? Explain.

COMPLETED
STUDENT
SHEETS

Analyzing Fingerprints

4. Make a new fingerprint of your right index finger in the middle of the space below. Using a magnifying glass, identify and label its characteristics.

My Right Index Fingerprint

Answers will vary.

5. What pattern is it?
   Answers will vary.

6. Summarize your findings.
   Answers will vary, but there should be some reference to the various types of characteristics noted.

Analyzing Fingerprints

1. An example of a partially analyzed fingerprint is given below. Note the method of identifying a characteristic, labeling it in the margins, and drawing a line between the characteristic and the label.

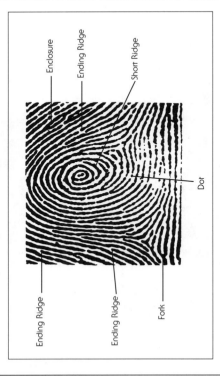

Ending Ridge

Enclosure

Ending Ridge

Short Ridge

Ending Ridge

Dot

Fork

2. Student Sheet 1.4 illustrates the three types of fingerprint patterns. The above fingerprint has what type pattern?
   It is a loop.

3. Student Sheet 1.5 illustrates the different types of characteristics. Referring to it, continue the analysis of the print above by identifying and labeling at least five other characteristics. (You do not have to use all five *types* of characteristics.)

Ten to Two

Number Systems

Decimal (Base 10)	Binary (Base 2)
$10^0 = 1$	$1 = 2^0 = 1_2$
$10^1 = 10$	$2 = 2^1 = 10_2$
$10^2 = 100$	$4 = 2^2 = 100_2$
$10^3 = 1000$	$8 = 2^3 = 1000_2$
$10^4 = 10000$	$16 = 2^4 = 10000_2$

Write the following numbers as sums of powers of 2 and then in base 2.

Base 10	Sums of Powers of 2	Base 2
1	2^0	1_2
2	2^1	10_2
3	$2^1 + 2^0$	11_2
4	2^2	100_2
5	$2^2 + 2^0$	101_2
6	$2^2 + 2^1$	110_2
7	$2^2 + 2^1 + 2^0$	111_2
8	2^3	1000_2
9	$2^3 + 2^0$	1001_2
10	$2^3 + 2^1$	1010_2
11	$2^3 + 2^1 + 2^0$	1011_2
12	$2^3 + 2^2$	1100_2
13	$2^3 + 2^2 + 2^0$	1101_2
14	$2^3 + 2^2 + 2^1$	1110_2
15	$2^3 + 2^2 + 2^1 + 2^0$	1111_2
16	2^4	10000_2

Base 10	Sums of Powers of 2	Base 2
17	$2^4 + 2^0$	10001_2
18	$2^4 + 2^1$	10010_2
19	$2^4 + 2^1 + 2^0$	10011_2
20	$2^4 + 2^2$	10100_2
21	$2^4 + 2^2 + 2^0$	10101_2
22	$2^4 + 2^2 + 2^1$	10110_2
23	$2^4 + 2^2 + 2^1 + 2^0$	10111_2
24	$2^4 + 2^3$	11000_2
25	$2^4 + 2^3 + 2^0$	11001_2
26	$2^4 + 2^3 + 2^1$	11010_2
27	$2^4 + 2^3 + 2^1 + 2^0$	11011_2
28	$2^4 + 2^3 + 2^2$	11100_2
29	$2^4 + 2^3 + 2^2 + 2^0$	11101_2
30	$2^4 + 2^3 + 2^2 + 2^1$	11110_2
31	$2^4 + 2^3 + 2^2 + 2^1 + 2^0$	11111_2
32	2^5	100000_2

Group Analysis

Fork
Fork
Ending Ridge
Fork
Ending Ridge
Enclosure
Enclosure
Short Ridge
Fork
Fork
Fork
Ending Ridge

1. As a group, analyze this print. Discuss any discrepancies and work toward consensus.

2. When all groups are ready, the class will discuss the process of analyzing a fingerprint to verify that all are using the same procedure. Be prepared to share your findings, particularly your methods to solve discrepancies.

COMPLETED STUDENT SHEET 4.1 (cont'd)

Ten to Two

Do the following problems in both the decimal system and the binary system.

Decimal System	Binary System
1. $16 + 8 = 24$	$10000_2 + 1000_2 = 11000_2$
2. $32 + 4 = 36$	$100000_2 + 100_2 = 100100_2$
3. $16 + 2 = 18$	$10000_2 + 10_2 = 10010_2$
4. $32 + 16 + 8 + 1 = 57$	$100000_2 + 10000_2 + 1000_2 + 1_2 = 111001_2$
5. $32 + 16 + 4 + 2 = 54$	$100000_2 + 10000_2 + 100_2 + 10_2 = 110110_2$
6. $32 + 16 + 8 + 4 + 2 + 1 = 63$	$100000_2 + 10000_2 + 1000_2 + 100_2 + 10_2 + 1_2 = 111111_2$
7. $31 - 1 = 30$	$11111_2 - 1_2 = 11110_2$
8. $16 - 2 = 14$	$10000_2 - 10_2 = 1110_2$
9. $13 - 3 = 10$	$1101_2 - 11_2 = 1010_2$
10. $18 - 1 = 17$	$1010_2 - 1_2 = 1001_2$

COMPLETED STUDENT SHEET 4.5

Binary Primary

1. Explain in writing why the Henry Primary Classification Fingerprint System is a binary system whether one uses base 10 or base 2 numerals. Use examples of encoding and decoding primary classifications to support your argument. *Answers will vary, but the essence is to understand that the classification is based on two possible outcomes—a presence or absence of a whorl. This is analogous to a light switch that has two possible positions—on or off. Each position can be represented by a different symbol, two symbols in all. A numeration system based on two symbols is called a binary system. The Henry Primary Classification System can be represented with two symbols, 1 for presence of a whorl, 0 for absence of a whorl. The system is binary; even though Henry chose to use more symbols, he could have classified a set of fingerprints using just two symbols.*

2. Explain what type of system would be needed to incorporate information on all three types of fingerprint patterns—whorls, loops, and arches. *Answers will vary. There are many creative solutions. One, and maybe the least creative, would use W, L, and A or 1, 2, and 3 for the symbols, and use position left to right to represent the fingers 1 to 10.*

LAW Summary

Write a brief statement describing your findings regarding the frequency of LAW (loops, arches, and whorls) by gender and by finger. Hypothesize how these findings might be used by the law (police).

Answers will vary, but should be consistent with the class data. Students could also make reference to the approximate distributions found in the general population, particularly if there were any great differences.

There are various uses of fingerprints mentioned in the Writing Link "Other Uses for Fingerprinting." Students are asked to come up with more ideas.

Cores, Deltas, and Ridges

1. Every loop has a core, one delta, and ridges. Examine the loop below. Do the following:
   a. Find the core—the center ridge.
   b. Find the delta—that point on a ridge at or in front of and nearest the center of the divergence of the type lines.
   c. Determine the ridge count—the number of ridges between the core and the ridge that forms the delta.

Core

Delta

7 Ridges

2. Using a magnifying glass, examine one of your fingerprints that is a loop. Locate its core, its delta, and determine the ridge count.

Finger Number	Ridge Count
Answers will vary.	

3. When you have finished, trade fingerprints with a member of your group. Determine the new fingerprint's ridge count.

Name of Group Member	Finger Number	Ridge Count
Answers will vary.		

4. Check each other's work.

NCIC FPC and Me

1. The NCIC FPC consists of a twenty-digit code made up of ten two-digit codes, one for each of the ten fingers. The code is read from left to right, beginning with the two-digit code for finger 1 and proceeding in order to the two-digit code for finger 10.

Name	Chris Tyler																			
NCIC FPC	A	A	5	7	P	I	0	9	T	T	0	4	C	M	D	0	0	6	5	5

a. Determine the fingerprint pattern on each of Chris's fingers.

	1 Thumb	2 Index	3 Middle	4 Ring	5 Little
Right Hand	A 16	L(R) 16	W 8	L (U) 8	A 4

	6 Thumb	7 Index	8 Middle	9 Ring	10 Little
Left Hand	L (U) 4	W 2	W 2	L(U) 1	L(R) 1

b. Calculate Chris's decimal primary classification.

$$\frac{2+1}{8+2+1} = \frac{3}{11}$$

2. Determine your NCIC FPC and complete the NCIC FPC form below. It is sometimes difficult to differentiate the various whorl patterns. Consult with your group members and refer to Student Sheet 6.2 to help in making any difficult decisions.
   Answers will vary.

Name										
NCIC FPC										

3. When you have finished, exchange papers with a classmate and check each other's work.